The Story of China

Miriam Greenblatt

Don-chean Chu
Professor of Comparative Education
Indiana University of Pennsylvania

Series Editor
Kimball Wiles
Formerly Dean, School of Education
University of Florida, Gainesville

McCormick-Mathers Publishing Company, Inc.
Cincinnati, Ohio 45202

Acknowledgment is made to Harper & Row, Publishers, Inc., for permission to quote passages from Cheng Ing Kwei's diary on pages 102-103 in *East of Home*, by Santha Rama Rau, copyright 1950 by Santha Rama Rau; and to Victor Gollancz, Ltd., London, for British and Open Market rights to reprint these passages.

The symbols used to indicate the pronunciation of Chinese words in this text are based on the diacritical system used in *Webster's New Elementary Dictionary*, copyright 1965 by G. & C. Merriam Co. Publishers of the Merriam-Webster Dictionaries. The phonetic system of modern Chinese, or Mandarin, is comparatively simple and regular. Thus the following consonants *p, t, k, ch,* and *ts* are regularly pronounced *b, d, g, j,* and *dz*. However, when these consonants are followed by an apostrophe, they are pronounced as in normal English. For example, *Ch'in* is pronounced *chin* but *Chin* becomes *jin*. Other examples of pronunciation include *eng*, which becomes *ung;* and *hs*, which becomes *sh* as in *Hsien Feng* (ʹshe-ʹen ʹfung); *ih* which becomes *ir* as in *shih* (*shir*); and *ou* which becomes o as in Chou (jō).

Maps and Charts by
  Graphic Presentation Services

Drawings by
  Staff Artist

Copyright © 1968 by
  McCormick-Mathers Publishing Company, Inc.

Philippines copyright 1968 by
  McCormick-Mathers Publishing Company, Inc.

VH 10 9 8 7 6 5 4 3 2

All rights reserved. No part of this work covered by the copyrights hereon may be reproduced or used in any form or by any means, graphic, electronic, or mechanical, including photocopying, recording, taping, or by information storage and retrieval systems without written permission from the publisher. Manufactured in the United States of America.

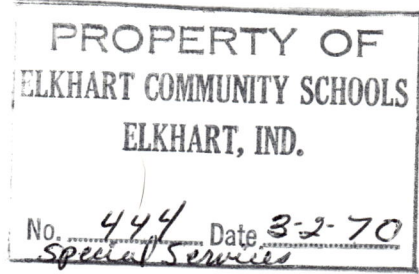

Table of Contents

The Long March	iv
Unit 1 — Life in Old China	6
Unit 2 — The Home of the Chinese People	30
Unit 3 — The Arts of Civilization	46
Unit 4 — The Passing of Old China	68
Unit 5 — Under the Red Star	91
Unit 6 — Formosa and the Nationalists	122
Unit 7 — China and the Road Ahead	136
Glossary	153
Index	155

The Long March

Their black eyes wide with eagerness, a group of young students enters the great exhibition hall. Quickly they line up along the side wall. As soon as they are in place, the teen-aged girl guide standing in front of the wall presses her finger against a button.

"Oo-ooh!" The sound is an admiring gasp from the group as a giant map on the wall lights up. Then all is quiet. The students bend forward to hear every word that the guide is saying. The story she will tell, they know, is the story of the "Long March." The wall map shows the route of the march.

The time was October, 1934. China was in the midst of a civil war. Two groups were struggling for control of the nation's government. One group was called the Nationalists. The other group was called the Communists.

Nationalist troops had surrounded Communist headquarters in the southeast part of China. Day by day they had moved in closer and drawn their ring of soldiers tighter and tighter. Tens of thousands of Communists had died in battle. It seemed only a matter of time before the Nationalists would strike the final blow.

But the blow was never struck. Instead the Communists broke through the ring of Nationalist troops that surrounded them. They set out on foot for the north of China, where they hoped to establish new headquarters in a safer place.

The Communist Red Army numbered 100,000 men at the start of the Long March. They were armed with knives, ancient rifles, homemade grenades, and only a few modern weapons. Most of the soldiers were young, in their late teens and early twenties. Some were accompanied by wives and children. They carried bags of rice, cooking pots, and a few extra clothes. Heavier articles such as spinning wheels, blacksmith tools, sewing machines, and plows were packed on donkeys and mules.

For one year the Communists made their way west and then north. They climbed high mountains where the air was so thin that it was a struggle to breathe. They built bamboo bridges across narrow valleys thousands of feet deep. They pushed through gloomy forests and deep swamps, across flooded rivers and snow-covered mountain ranges.

The Communists were followed most of the way by Nationalist forces, who bombed and machine-gunned them from the air. There were frequent battles between the two armies. Sometimes the Communists also had to fight local tribesmen, who viewed all strangers within their territory as enemies. The Communists endured heat and cold, disease and a shortage of food. Many died.

In October, 1935, the remnants of the Red Army finally reached their destination in northern China. The ragged, exhausted marchers had traveled more than 6,000 miles. Only 20,000—one in five—had lived through it all. But the survivors were full of pride. They had overcome all the obstacles set up by man and nature. They had completed the Long March!

By December, 1936, the Communists had established new headquarters near the town of Yenan. There they scooped caves out of the hills to serve as homes. They planted fields with cabbages and millet. As they worked, the Communist leaders made plans to continue their struggle against the Nationalists. No one would have thought this group of cave dwellers would, in just thirteen years' time, rule the entire mainland of China.

As the guide ends the story, the lights on the wall map go out. The young students stand quietly for a moment. Then they move on, and a new group enters the hall.

The exhibition hall is part of the Museum for Chinese History and the Revolution, in China's capital of Peking. The Museum with its lighted wall map is the only one in China. The Long March itself, however, is China's most popular subject for exhibitions. Every school and factory in the nation contains some kind of model or map showing the route the Red Army followed. Every village hall contains pictures of the Red Army's leaders and of the caves in which the army lived after it reached northern China.

The story of the Long March reaches the Chinese people in other ways, too. It is a popular subject for movies, plays, and operas. School children learn folk songs about the Red Army's courage. Artists paint pictures of the march.

As you learn about what led up to the Long March, you will understand why the Communist government of China considers it so important. But before you do this, there is another and very different "Long March" to learn about. It is the history of the Chinese over the past 5,000 years.

In our Long March through China's history we will learn about its beginnings in a river valley thousands of years ago. We will follow the Chinese people as they developed a splendid civilization long before nations were thought of in Europe or America. We will read about their great engineering feats, such as the Great Wall and the Grand Canal. And we will read about the great inventions they gave to the world—paper and paper money, gunpowder and silk, porcelain and printing.

This book will tell of Confucius, a wise man whose teachings influenced the Chinese family and the Chinese government for 2,000 years. It will also tell of a prince who united China and established the Chinese empire and of other rulers, some of whom were foreigners. Foreign invaders there were who conquered and ruled. But the Chinese people always kept their identity and, in time, the foreigners either were overthrown or adopted Chinese ways.

As the story proceeds, we will meet Marco Polo, a European who traveled across Asia to China in the late 1200's. It was Marco's glowing tales of the riches and accomplishments of the Chinese that sparked the interest of people

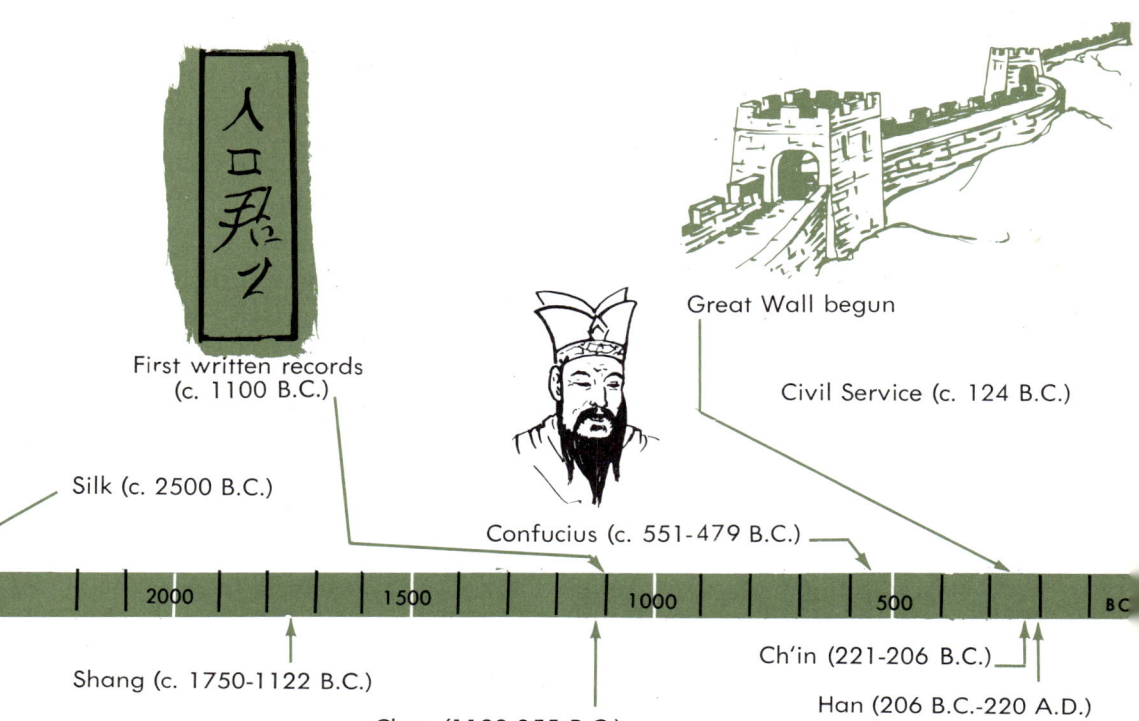

in Europe. As time went on, Western European traders succeeded in reaching China by sea. Earliest of the sea traders were the Portuguese, who came in the 1500's. British and other traders followed soon after.

At first trade between China and Western Europe was limited, for the Chinese did not think the Europeans had much to offer them. Also, the Chinese looked upon all foreigners as barbarians. They wanted to keep them out so that China could continue in its accustomed ways. But this was not to be. By the 1800's Western Europe's demand for trade finally led to war and China's defeat.

As the Chinese government weakened, foreigners gained many special rights in the country. This made the Chinese

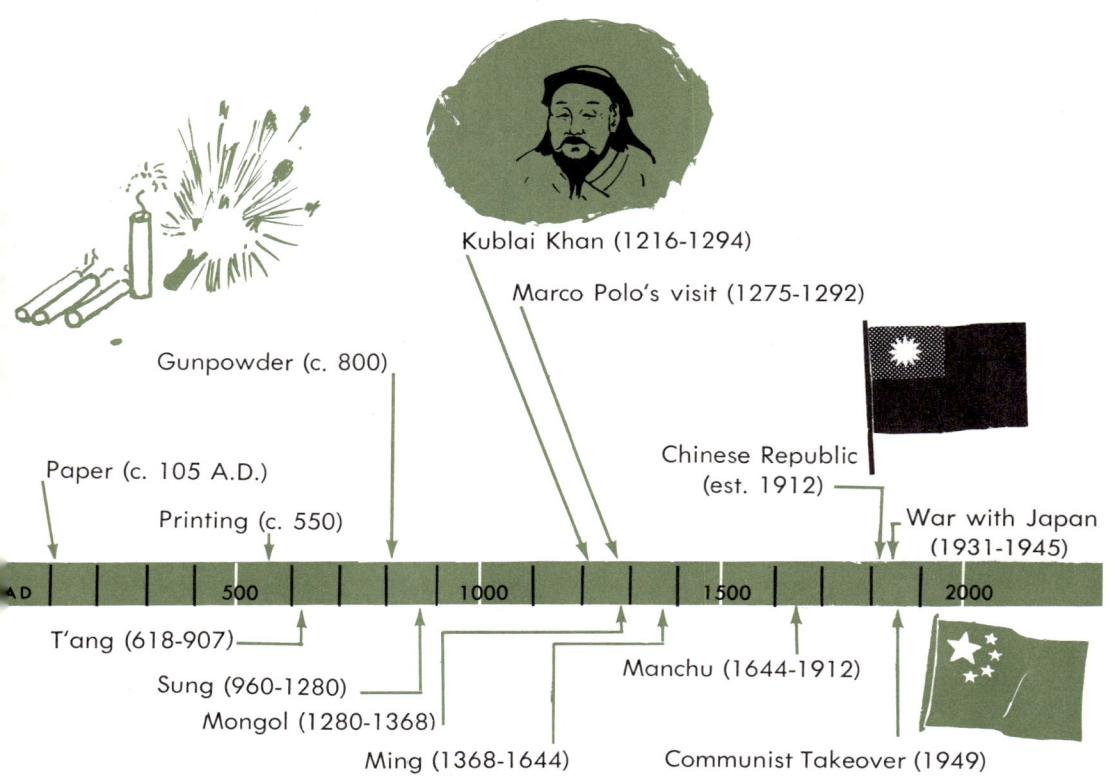

unhappy because they were no longer masters in their own land. In addition, floods and droughts brought widespread hunger, and there were many peasant uprisings. Changing China had many problems.

Finally we see the downfall of the 2,000-year-old Chinese empire and the rise of the Nationalists. The Nationalists set up a republic. But they had difficulties in meeting the needs of all the people. Japan invaded China and a great war engulfed the nation. This prepared the way for the rise of the Communists. The Communists, as we have seen, took over the government in 1949.

Now you are ready to begin your Long March through the pages of this book.

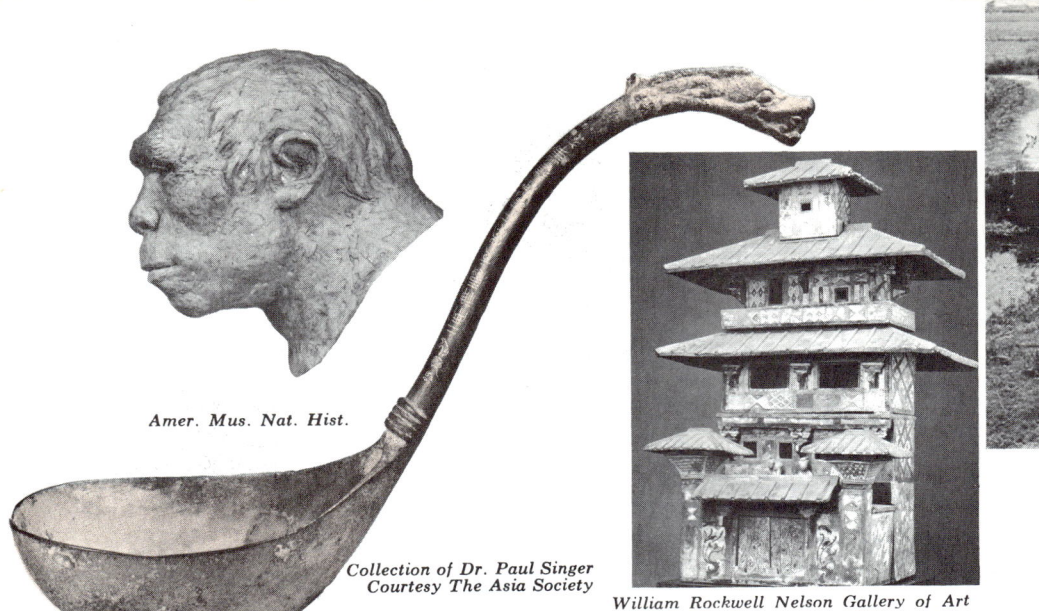

Amer. Mus. Nat. Hist.

*Collection of Dr. Paul Singer
Courtesy The Asia Society*

*William Rockwell Nelson Gallery of Art
Atkins Museum of Fine Arts*

Peking man, an ancestor of the Chinese people, lived about one million years ago. The food ladle at the left dates back to 1500 B.C.

UNIT 1 Life in

One of the most important things to remember about China is that it is very old. This country in eastern Asia has a civilization that dates back longer than that of any other country in the world.

THE OLDEST LIVING CIVILIZATION

The Chinese civilization began about 3,000 B.C. (before Christ) in a river valley in northern China. The first inhabitants of the valley had been wandering hunters and fishermen. After they learned to farm, they did not need to roam about in search of food. They could settle down in

Eastfoto

The Chinese made pottery in early times. The pottery model of a nobleman's house, at left, is 2,000 years old. The vase shown here is an early example of porcelain, which the Chinese were first to perfect. Old China made many gifts to the world. One of these was rice, a basic food crop. Another was the good drink called tea. Both products, shown above, grow in Asia, where they had their beginnings.

A.M.N.H.

William Rockwell Nelson Gallery of Art Atkins Museum of Fine Arts

Old China

permanent homes and tend their crops. Even more important, they could develop cities and government, temples and writing, coin money, and devise a calendar. As the years passed, the Chinese people grew in numbers and spread out over a vast area. Their way of life became one of the finest the world has ever known.

A Look at the Land

Why did people build homes and develop the arts of living in this land of China so many centuries ago? One answer can be found, perhaps, in the soil and climate of the valley where the civilization began.

7

The valley is known as the Yellow River valley after the Yellow River, or **Hwang Ho** \ʹhwang-ʹhō\, which flows through it. The yellow soil of the valley is deep, has no stones, and is rich in plant-building elements. The early people living in the valley found it excellent for farming, provided they could get enough water.

Sometimes enough rain for crops fell on the yellow earth. At other times the people had to bring water to the fields by means of irrigation canals. They also had to keep the Yellow River and its tributaries from flooding. Work of this kind could not be done by a few men working on their own. It could only be done by large numbers of men working together under some kind of central direction.

The farmers in the Yellow River valley were able to grow enough food for themselves and their families and also have some to spare. At the same time they had to work hard for their food supply, and they had learned to cooperate with their neighbors. Under these conditions, say many scholars, the Chinese civilization arose.

In the Beginning

At first the people in the Yellow River valley lived in caves in the ground. They dug their homes out of the yellow earth and piled straw on top of wooden beams to serve as roofs. The entrances to the houses were at the top. The houses were warm in winter and cool in summer, and they protected people against the dust storms that often swirled across the land. The fields of grain and vegetables were nearby, where they could be tended and guarded from prowling animals. The farmers used hoes with stone blades to work the fertile soil.

In addition to farming, the early Chinese fished in the Yellow River and its tributaries, first with spears, later with nets. They also kept pigs and hunted wild animals—

bears, boar, deer, and foxes. The animals gave them food and also skins from which to make clothing. The Chinese hunted with arrows and knives of bone or stone. They used stone knives to cut up the meat and to scrape the skins to prepare them for clothing. In other words, they were living in the Stone Age.

As time went on, the Chinese developed hemp from a wild plant, spun its strong fibers into thread, and wove the thread into cloth. They learned to make pottery from clay and to shape it on a wheel. Pottery vessels were a great aid in carrying water and in cooking food and storing it. After a while the Chinese began to decorate their pottery with pictures of animals and other designs. They made jewelry from shells and played music on whistles.

By the year 2,000 B.C. the Chinese had spread out to the east and south. They drained marshes and planted the land with grain. They added hearths to their houses and built earth walls around their villages for protection. They learned how to raise cattle, horses, and sheep. They also learned how to make silk.

The Chinese mined copper and tin and mixed the two metals to make **bronze.** Tools and weapons made of bronze were better shaped and sharper than the stone tools were. Bronze could be shaped into axes, swords, knives, and many kinds of vessels. It could also be used to make ornaments and even stoves. The Chinese had progressed from the Stone Age and entered the Bronze Age.

This bronze vessel was found deep in the earth on the site of an ancient city in China. It is about 3,000 years old.

Avery Brundage Collection
Courtesy The Asia Society

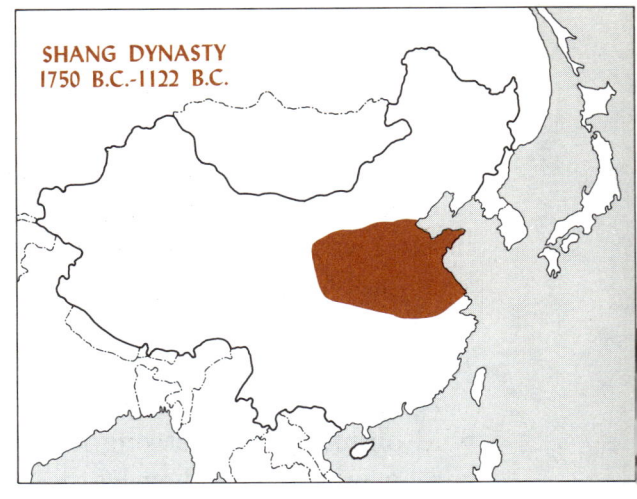

China's oldest records date back to the Shang kingdom, shown in color on this map. Compare the area with that of China today, shown in the heavy surrounding outline on the map.

The Shang Kingdom

Our earliest historical records of Chinese life date from relics that have survived from the Bronze Age. **Archaeologists** \ˌär-kē-'äl-ə-jəsts\, or scientists who dig in the earth to learn about the past, discovered the remains of a Bronze Age city near present-day **Anyang** \'än-yang\. This ancient city was one of the capitals of the **Shang** \shäng\ kingdom, so-called from the name of its ruling family. A succession of rulers from the same family is known as a **dynasty** \'dī-nə-stē\. The Shang dynasty lasted from about 1750 B.C. to about 1122 B.C.

The remains of the Shang city show that the ruling class lived in palaces with wooden pillars supporting the roof and walls built of earth or brick. Like many buildings in northern China today, the palaces faced south to get as much sun as possible during the cold winter months. The members of the ruling class were warriors and also hunted in chariots.

The other people apparently lived in the same kind of underground houses they had used during the Stone Age. Most were farmers. But some were highly skilled craftsmen who made splendid articles out of bronze. The Shang bronzes found by archaeologists are considered the finest the world has ever seen.

The people of the Shang kingdom also left behind the oldest form of Chinese writing yet found. It was carved mostly on pieces of cattle bone and on tortoise shells. This ancient writing later developed into the writing system the Chinese adopted about 2,200 years ago and still use today. It was their writing system, more than any of their other arts, that helped hold the Chinese people together on their Long March through history. The spoken language changed from place to place as the centuries passed. But the written language stayed the same. Every educated Chinese was able to read the works of Chinese authors and scholars whenever they had been written.

China During the Chou Dynasty

The next family to rule China after the Shang dynasty was called **Chou** \'jō\. Few of the Chou kings were strong rulers. As a result, during much of this time China was divided into small states. The lords, or rulers, of these states swore loyalty to the Chou king but paid him little attention. They spent most of their time warring with other states. This finally weakened the dynasty.

During the Chou dynasty the ways of living of the people changed. Farmers in north China no longer lived underground. Some dug caves out of hillsides. But most of them lived in houses made of packed earth or sundried bricks. The houses stood beside dirt roads and were protected by mud walls. In the harvest season the roofs were piled high with wheat and millet and other grains. The farmers heated their houses by burning straw and brush. To take full advantage of the fire, they built **k'angs** \kangz\, or wide brick shelves, several feet above the fire and used them as beds. How nice it was to fall asleep on the heated bricks! Unfortunately, the fire would die down during the night, the bricks would lose their heat, and people would wake up shivering with cold.

The lords of the various Chinese states and other members of the ruling class lived in towns. The towns were square in shape and were surrounded by walls made of pounded earth. Around each wall was a wide ditch filled with water. Gates in the wall were opened during the day and closed at night. On either side of a gate was a watchtower manned by soldiers.

Town houses were made of wood, usually painted a bright color. Each town had an altar where the lord made offerings to the local God of the Soil. Each town also had a market place, for trade was lively during the Chou dynasty. Merchants traveled from town to town visiting the markets. They carried their wares of silk cloth and copper vessels on pack oxen or in ox-drawn carts. Coined money came into use.

During the Chou dynasty some Chinese moved southward from the Yellow River valley into the valley of the **Yangtze Kiang** \\'yang-,sē ki-'ang\\, or Yangtze River. There rain was plentiful, and the climate was warm enough for two crops a year. Farmers were able to grow an abundance of food. Many villages and towns sprang up along the river's course. The people lived mostly in houses made either of mud brick or of woven **bamboo.** Bamboo is a treelike grass that grows as high as 40 feet. Its stem is stiff and hollow. The Chinese used bamboo for making arrows, books, carrying poles, tow ropes, bridges, rafts, sails for ships, and furniture as well as houses.

Families and Ancestors

Most important in Old China was the family. People's names showed this. First came the family name, then the individual name. For example, Sun Yat-sen was a member of the Sun family. Yat-sen was his personal name.

If you were the oldest man in a Chinese family, you were the head of the household. You managed whatever property the family owned. You had complete control over your children and were usually very strict with them. You even had the right, as their father, to condemn a son or daughter to death for misbehaving. You decided the occupation your sons would follow and whom your children would marry. When you became too old to work, your sons were expected to support and care for you. Old age was greatly respected in China because old people were believed to have gained wisdom by living.

Old age was also respected because older people would soon be **ancestors** \'an-,ses-tərz\. The Chinese believed that people became spirits after death and went right on living in another world. They believed that these ancestor spirits could either help them or harm them, depending on whether or not they performed special memorial services. So once or twice a year, Chinese families would take offerings to the graves of their ancestors to show that they were always remembered.

Confucius and the Chinese Way

The person who had the greatest influence on the Chinese way of life was the man we call **Confucius** \kən'fyü-shəs\. His Chinese name was **Kung Fu-tzu** \'küng 'fü-'dzü\, or Kung the Master. We use the Latin form of his name because the Europeans who first studied his teachings had trouble pronouncing the Chinese form.

Confucius was born about 551 B.C. of a poor upper-class family. When he was three, his father died. Encouraged by his mother, he worked his way through school. He learned

Sayings of Confucius

Duty to parents is the root of all virtue.

To see the right and not do it is to be a coward.

It is only the very wisest and the very stupidest who never change.

Not to withdraw after making an error is itself a new error.

What you do not want done to yourself do not do to others.

Meet evil with justice. Meet good with good.

his lessons well, and he especially liked to read early Chinese history and poetry. As a result, he came to believe that people ought to follow the old customs carefully.

In his late teens and early twenties Confucius held several offices in the government of his state. He was not satisfied with politics, however, so at 22 he set himself up as a teacher. He taught government, history, mathematics, music, poetry, and sports. His reputation as a teacher grew steadily, and people came from all parts of China to study with him.

Confucius taught for about twenty-five years. But he did not forget his early experiences in government. Also, he worried a great deal about the continuous fighting between the Chinese states. He gave serious thought to the importance of good government, and he developed ideas about how men could learn to live together peaceably.

As Confucius grew older, he became more and more eager to put his ideas into practice. Finally he left teaching and began to travel about China. For 13 years he visited one state after another. In each, he offered the lord advice on how to become a better ruler. In each, the lord smiled po- itely and rejected Confucius's services.

At last Confucius returned to his home state. There he reopened his school and spent the last years of his life teaching and editing books. He died at the age of 73.

Confucius did not receive great honors while he was alive. After his death, however, people began to realize what a wise man he had been. They put his sayings into textbooks that school boys were expected to learn by heart. They gave examinations based on his teachings. Passing these examinations was the way to become a high public official.

Old China had other wise men who also set up schools. But none had as great an influence on Chinese life as did Confucius. **Confucianism** was not a religion, but Confucius came to be respected almost as a god. In later years temples were built to him in the principal cities. And for 2,000 years people followed his teachings as if they were scriptures.

The Birth of an Empire

A few years after the end of the Chou dynasty Prince Cheng, ruler of the state called Ch'in, rose to great power. He made war on the other states. By 221 B.C. he had become the supreme ruler of the land. He changed his name

The ancient Chinese built temples in which to worship the gods. The Temple of Heaven, below, is in Peking. Temples were also built to honor Confucius.
Amer. Mus. Nat. Hist.

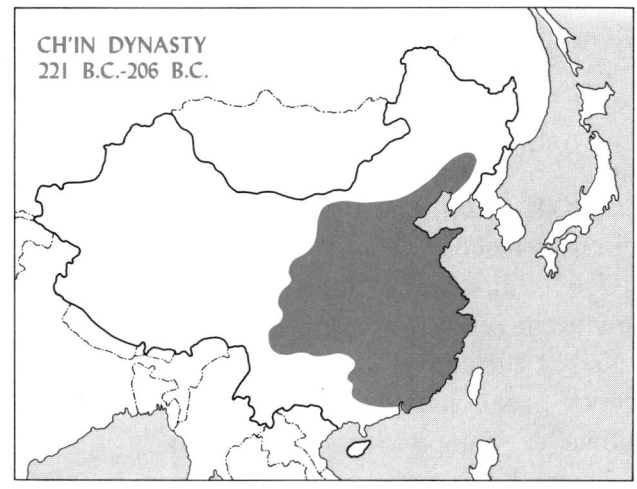

China became an empire in the reign of Ch'in, a strong ruler who came to power in 221 B.C. He extended China and built the Great Wall as a protection against warriors from the north.

to **Shih Huang Ti** \'shir-'hwäng 'tē\, or the First Emperor, and declared China an empire. We get the name China from Ch'in.

Shih Huang Ti did many things to unify China. He insisted that all businessmen use the same coins and the same system of weights and measures. He ordered scholars everywhere to use the same writing system. He had the walls that separated some states torn down. He also began the building of the Great Wall to protect China's northern frontier against invasion.

One day Shih Huang Ti gave an order that shocked the people greatly. He did not want his subjects to read books with ideas that were different from his. So he ordered a book burning. Only books in his own collection and those on farming, fortune telling, and medicine were to be saved. Hundreds of thousands of volumes went up in smoke. Scholars who objected were either sent away or buried alive.

This attempt at thought control deeply disturbed Chinese scholars. But they kept in mind one of Confucius's teachings, namely, that ideas are stronger than force. They saved some of the books by burying them under trees or putting them in deep wells. They memorized others.

Several years after Shih Huang Ti died, the son who succeeded him was overthrown by a revolt. The revolt was

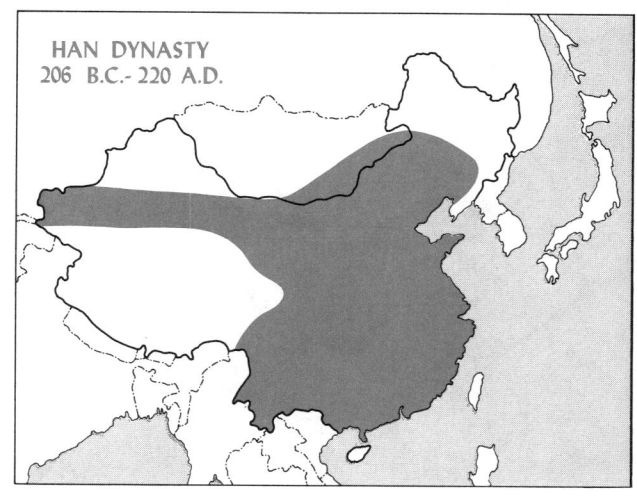

The Han reign was a time when China prospered and developed many of the arts of civilization. How much did China increase in area under the rule of the Hans?

led by a peasant who organized the farmers into a strong army. This dynasty, which was called **Han**\hän\, lasted until 220 A.D. During the Han dynasty many of the old books were once again read and copied.

Changing Dynasties

The Han emperors accomplished a great deal during their reign. They set up a system of government under which China was ruled for 2,000 years. They made Confucius's teachings the law of the land. They extended the nation's boundaries to the west and south. Under the Hans the Chinese invented paper and porcelain. They also developed a rich trade with the far-off Roman empire. The Han reign was so great and glorious that many Chinese today call themselves "Sons of Han."

Dynasties came and went. Once again the empire was divided, and war ravaged the land. Tribes from the north invaded China and overran the Yellow River valley. Life became difficult for the Chinese people and many turned for comfort to **Buddhism** \'bü-diz-əm\, a religion brought by missionaries from India. They responded to the hope held out by Buddhism of inner peace and heavenly salvation. China became a stronghold of Buddhism after it grew weak in India.

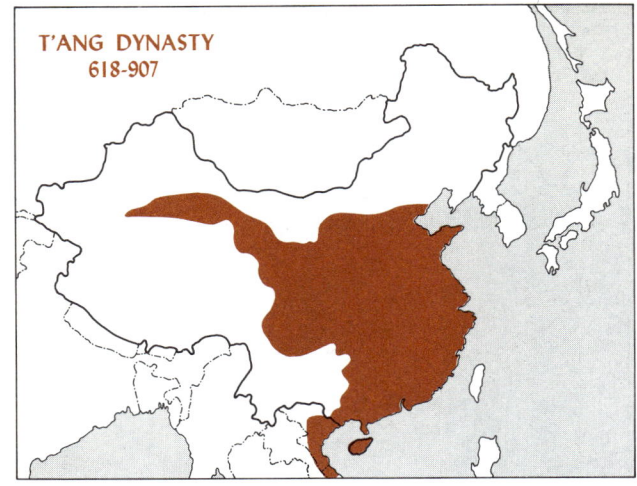

In the T'ang period China had a golden age of art and invention. Confucius's teachings became the basis of examination for public office.

After a time the empire was again united, and peace came to the country. Under the T'ang and Sung dynasties the emperors were often men of culture as well as military might. They encouraged poets, painters, and sculptors to produce. Trade flourished, aided by the development of paper money. Printing and gunpowder were invented.

The Mongol Invasion

During the late 1200's China was invaded. Out of the grasslands to the north rode the **Mongols** \ˈmän-gōlz\. Unlike the Chinese, who were mostly farmers and small businessmen, the Mongols were **nomads** \ˈnō̇ˈmadz\ who herded sheep. Nomads are people who move from place to place seeking food and water for themselves and their animals.

Because the Mongols spent so much time moving around, they were excellent horsemen. It is said that a Mongol could stay in the saddle for ten days and nights at a time. The settled Chinese farmers were no match for the swift-moving Mongol horsemen. Gradually the Mongols took over more and more of China. Finally, in 1280, the Mongol leader **Kublai Khan** \ˌkü-ˌblī-ˈkän\ became China's foreign ruler.

The Mongol dynasty lasted until 1368. A notable event of this dynasty was the arrival of the first European visitors to China. The Europeans were the Polo brothers, merchants from the Italian city of Venice. On their second visit, Marco Polo, the teen-aged son of one of the brothers, accompanied them. Four years later they reached China and met the emperor. Kublai Khan took a liking to bright young Marco and sent him on errands to different parts of the empire. After 17 years in China the Polos returned to Venice. Their visit to China was important because of Marco Polo's book in which he told of his experiences. In the book he described the splendors of Kublai Khan's court and the high civilization that the Chinese had developed. The book sparked the interest of European traders in China.

The Mongol empire under Kublai Khan contained China and reached across Asia into Europe to include part of Russia.

The Ming period was a time of good government, and art was encouraged. Sculptured stone lions, like those shown in the picture, lined the highway going to the Ming tombs.

Charles Phelps Cushing

The Later Dynasties

After they had ruled for about 100 years, the Mongol rule was overthrown by a Chinese army. The founder of the dynasty, which was called **Ming,** was the son of a poor worker. The Ming emperors founded many schools and libraries. They also built splendid palaces and tombs.

After the Mings came the **Manchus** \'man-chüz\. Like the Mongols, the Manchus were not Chinese. They came from an area northeast of the Yellow Plain. They were invited into China after the last Ming emperor was overthrown by a revolt. This take-over was fairly easy because the Manchus were already familiar with the Chinese way of life.

The rule of the Mings and the first half of the Manchus was the most stable, or unchanging, period in China's history. From the middle of the 1300's to the early 1800's, it seemed as if time stood still in China. Except for a few years the country was at peace. The family was the center of everyday life, and the sayings of Confucius were taught in all the schools. No new ideas or inventions disturbed the even flow of the years. Scholars spent their time studying the old records and glorifying the achievements of the past. Other nations were almost completely ignored. The Chinese became more and more convinced that all foreigners were barbarians and that their way of life was the only civilized way to live.

The Challenge of the Europeans

Unfortunately for China, the outside world was not standing still. While the Chinese expected that the future would be exactly like the past, Europe was becoming modern. New nations arose. Explorers sailed to all parts of the world. People learned how to use the power of steam in place of muscles, wind, and water power. And everywhere factories were built which turned out vast quantities of manufactured goods.

By the early 1800's Europe's new ideas and inventions began to challenge the Chinese way of life. Against their will life was to change for the Chinese people, and Old China was to come to an end.

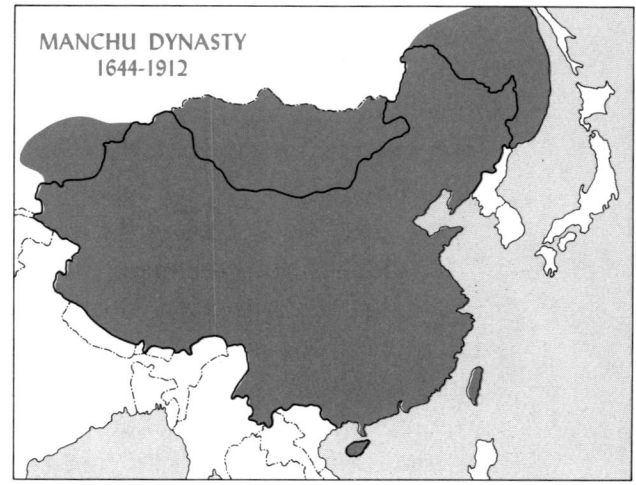

The Manchu empire had an area about as large as China today. The Manchu emperors were the last to sit on the Chinese throne.

FAMILY LIFE IN OLD CHINA

People in Old China were divided into two classes. One was the upper class, or gentry, whose members lived mostly in the towns and cities. The other was the lower class, whose people were mostly villagers. Government officials, scholars, and landlords usually belonged to the upper class. Farmers and craftsmen usually belonged to the lower class.

A Gentry Family

The home of the **Wang** \wäng\ family was more like an apartment building than a house. It had to be, for the family was very large. It included Mr. and Mrs. Wang, their young daughter, their five sons and their wives, five sets of grandchildren, and two widowed aunts of Mrs. Wang. Some three dozen servants were also part of the household.

The Wang home consisted of several one-story houses surrounded by a wall. This area was called a **compound** \ˈkäm-pȧund\. Each of the larger houses was built around an open courtyard and had a kitchen, a sitting room, a dining room, and three or four bedrooms. All the courtyards were connected by passageways. Mr. and Mrs. Wang and their daughter lived in one house. Mrs. Wang's widowed aunts lived in another house. And each of the Wang sons, with their wives and children, had a house of his own. The servants lived in the smaller houses, which had no living rooms, only bedrooms and a kitchen.

In addition to the houses the Wang home included a large hall called the Ancestral Hall. Along one of the walls of this hall stood wooden tablets with lists of Mr. Wang's ancestors, going back five generations. When the Wang sons were growing up, Mr. Wang had often taken them into the Ancestral Hall. There he had told them about what the Wangs had done in the past to bring honor to the family.

Every New Year's Day all the Wangs gathered in the Ancestral Hall. They burned incense in front of the tablets and placed an offering of food on the family altar. Then they told their ancestors about the important events of the past year. Since they believed that a man remained part of his family after death, he was naturally still interested in what was going on.

As head of the Wang family, Mr. Wang made the final decision on all family affairs. He had chosen his sons' wives, selecting girls from families that were either rich or had members who were government officials. He had also decided what work his sons were to do. Two sons had jobs in the family's shipping business, moving rice along the Yangtze River. Two were teachers, a respected profession in Old China. And the fifth son, who wanted to be an official, was preparing to take the national examination.

Although the Wang family owned a shipping business, most of their wealth came from their large holdings of land. Mr. Wang owned about 200 acres, which he rented to tenant farmers.

Whatever Mr. Wang and his sons earned went to support the entire family. If one of the sons fell ill or become unemployed, he did not worry about the welfare of his wife and children. The other men in the family would care for them.

When Mr. Wang died, the family property would be divided among his five sons. The oldest son would then become the family head. It would be his duty to make the final decision on all family affairs. And it would be the duty of the other brothers to respect and obey him just as they had respected and obeyed their father.

While Mr. Wang made the important decisions for the family, Mrs. Wang ran the household. She saw to it that the maids swept the stone-paved courtyard and washed the family clothes in the nearby river. She made certain that every kitchen had enough brushwood or charcoal to keep the stoves going. She told her daughters-in-law what clothes to wear and scolded them if she did not like their behavior. Just as the sons would not dare to disobey their father, so the sons' wives would not dare to disobey their mother-in-law.

A Peasant Family

Mr. Li \lē\ was a rice farmer. He owned one and one-half acres of fertile land in a small river valley. He was fortunate that his land was a single field rather than being cut up in several strips. This meant that he did not waste time walking from one strip to another. In addition to the land, he had the right to use water from the river to irrigate his crops.

Mr. Li grew two crops of rice a year. First, he and his two sons would flood the field. They pumped the water onto the land with a water wheel worked by foot pedals. Hour after hour they pushed the pedals—left foot, right foot, left foot, right foot—until the entire field was covered with water.

They had no buffalo to do the plowing, so they took turns pulling their wooden plow. Back and forth they would go across the field until the soil had been churned into mud. Then back they went to the foot pedals, this time to drain the field.

After the field was drained, Mr. Li and his sons would sow rice seed very thickly on one part of the field. Slowly the rice plants would push their way above the ground. When they were ten to twelve inches high, the men would pull them up and separate them. Then they would set out the plants, one at a time, several inches apart through the field. After that they would flood the field again.

Several times during the growing season, Mr. Li and his sons would drain the water off the field. They would walk along the rows of rice, carefully plucking out every weed. Again they would reflood the field.

When the rice ripened, the men would cut the stalks with hand sickles and stack the rice in sheaves to dry in the sun. After the sheaves were dry, they would toss them from one bamboo basket to another. As the sheaves sailed through the air, the heavy grains of rice separated from the lighter chaff and fell in the basket. The stalks, or chaff, would be blown away by the wind. This process of removing the chaff from the grain is called winnowing.

Growing rice was slow and backbreaking work. It was dirty work, too. Sometimes it seemed to Mr. Li that he spent most of his life knee-deep in a sea of mud.

Then came the pleasant days of the year. Like New Year's Day, when the sky was filled with fireworks. Or like the market days in town, when Mr. Li sold his rice, bought salt, and exchanged the latest news with his neighbors. Sometimes a traveling storyteller came to town. He would sit in the market place and tell the farmers wondrous tales of spirits, and ancient heroes, and foxes that could take on human form.

Both of Mr. Li's sons lived with him, as did his widowed mother. The house had four rooms. In the middle was a kitchen. In one corner of the kitchen the Lis kept their chickens. On one side of the house was a bedroom where Mr. and Mrs. Li and their three young grandchildren slept. On the other side were two smaller bedrooms. Mr. Li's older son and his wife slept in one. Mr. Li's mother and his second, unmarried son slept in the other.

Everyone in the Li family worked. The men farmed. The women cooked, made clothes, and wove straw hats to add

Amer. Mus. Nat. Hist.

For hundreds of years Chinese farmers have processed rice as shown here. After the rice stalks have been cut, the hulls are loosened from the grain by hard pounding. The rice is then tossed into the air in flat baskets like the one in this picture. The dry hulls blow away and the rice kernels are caught in the basket. What is this process called?

to the family income. At planting time and at harvest time, they often worked side by side with the men in the fields. Mr. Li's mother took care of her grandchildren, sewed, and fed the chickens. When the children were six they, too, would be expected to help.

The Chinese Family

The Wang family and the Li family differed in certain ways. The Wang family was much larger than the Li family. Both families got most of their living from the land. The

Wangs, however, rented their land to tenants, while the Li family farmed their land themselves. The Wangs looked down on anyone who worked with his hands. To the Li family, working with one's hands was the natural thing to do. All the Wang men knew how to read and write. The Lis did not.

The families were alike, however, in following the teachings of Confucius. "The first of all virtues," according to Confucius, was being a good son. A son should always try to do his very best in everything because that would bring great joy to his parents. He should never be rude or dishonest because that would bring them shame.

Chinese families taught their children how to behave by example. They also taught them good conduct by telling stories. A favorite story was about a little boy named Meng. His parents were poor farmers who could not afford to buy mosquito netting. One night they went to bed after a hard day's work, but they could not sleep because the mosquitoes kept biting them. So Meng threw off his bedcovers inviting the mosquitoes to bite him instead of his parents.

The Wang family and the Li family were alike in another way, too. To both families, the welfare of the group was more important than the welfare of individuals. If a Chinese man had a choice of professions, he always followed the one that would help his family most. The same was true when a Chinese couple married. Marriages were arranged by the fathers, each of whom wanted to benefit his own family. Often a bride and groom did not meet each other until the wedding day.

A Chinese writer named **Lin Yutang** \'lin 'yü-'tang\ once compared the Chinese family to a great tree. Some branches might die out, he said. But others would come up, so that the tree itself would live forever.

Main Dynasties in Chinese History

SHANG (c. 1750-1122 B.C.): A farming civilization that grew up in the Yellow River valley, developed a writing system, made splendid bronze articles, and used chariots in war.

CHOU (c. 1122-255 B.C.): The kings of this dynasty extended their rule southward into the Yangtze Valley. Confucius and other teachers lived during the second half of this dynasty.

CH'IN (221-206 B.C.): This short-lived but strong dynasty brought eastern China under control and established the empire.Shih Huang Ti, the founder, began building the Great Wall.

HAN (206 B.C.-A.D. 220): This dynasty vastly extended China's borders, had wide trade relations, and established a government based on Confucius's teachings that lasted 2,000 years. Many Chinese call themselves "Sons of Han."

SUI (589-618): Its strong rulers recovered lost territory for China and built most of the vast inland waterway called the Grand Canal.

T'ANG (618-907): In its early years this dynasty expanded its rule deep into Asia. Poets and painters were encouraged.

SUNG (960-1280): Its emperors unified China after a period of disorder. Art was encouraged. Paper money aided trade.

MONGOL (1280-1368): The Mongols, who controlled much of Asia and Europe, established China's capital at Peking. The most famous of the Mongol emperors was Kublai Khan.

MING (1368-1644): Under this native dynasty, art flourished. Great fleets went abroad to obtain tribute and trade.

MANCHU (1644-1912): The Manchus, invaders from the North, conquered China and expanded the empire. They were overthrown by a revolution, led by Sun Yat-sen.

I. **Word Study**

Match each word in **Column 1** with its meaning in **Column 2**.

Column 1
1. ancestors
2. archaeologist
3. bamboo
4. Buddhism
5. compound
6. Confucianism
7. dynasty
8. k'ang
9. nomads

Column 2
a. A wide brick shelf used as a bed
b. A succession of rulers from the same family
c. People who wander from place to place without a permanent home
d. Teachings of one of China's wise men
e. A religion that began in India
f. A tall grass with stiff, hollow stems
g. Forefathers
h. A scientist who digs in the earth to learn about the past
i. A group of houses inside a wall

II. **Reviewing What You Have Learned**

Make two columns on your paper under the headings: **A Gentry Family** and **A Peasant Family.** Then list the statements below under the proper headings. Some statements belong in both columns.

a. Three generations live together in the same house.
b. The men earn their living by farming.
c. Children are expected to obey their parents without question.
d. Boys learn to read and write.
e. Sons do the same kind of work as their fathers.
f. The family is more important than the individual.
g. People pay honor to their ancestors.

III. **Can You Explain?**

1. How Confucius influenced Chinese ways of living.
2. Why Marco Polo's visit was important in China's history.

PEOPLE'S REPUBLIC OF CHINA

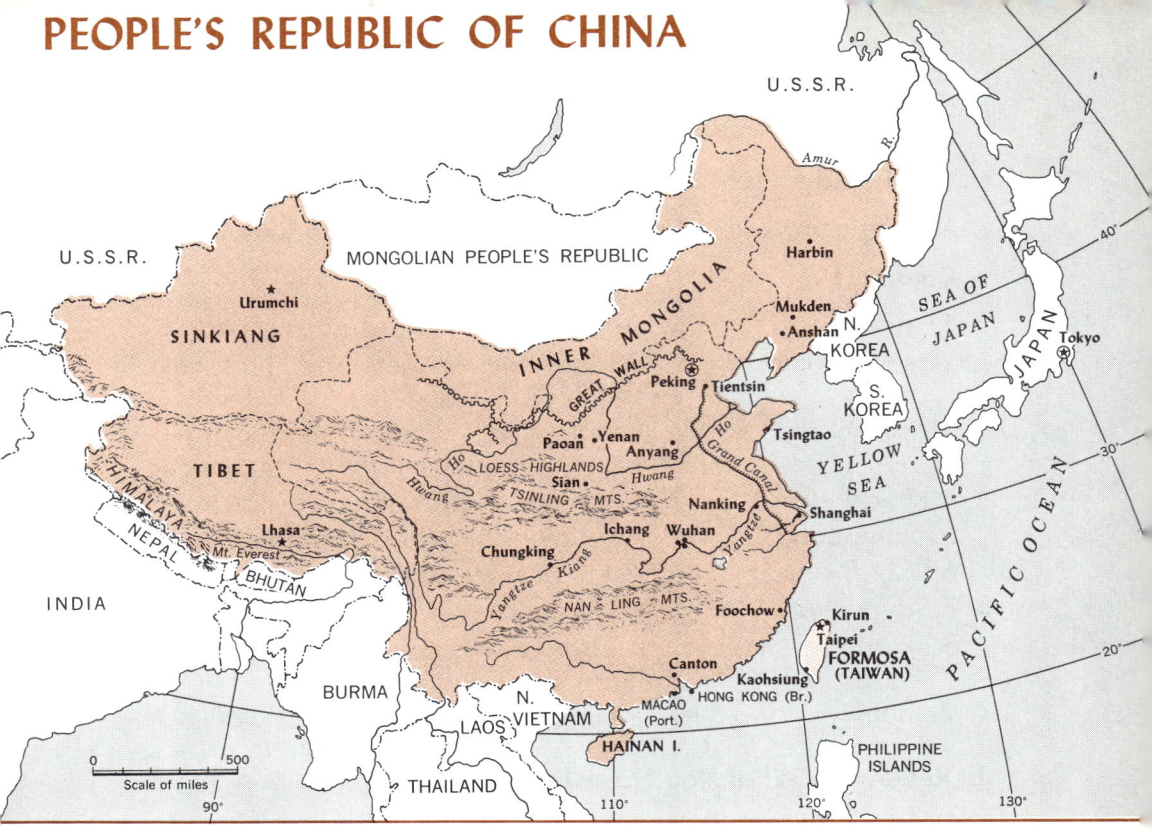

UNIT 2

The Home of the

Because geography has played an important part in the life of the Chinese, let us look at their homeland. Over the centuries the nation's boundaries have changed greatly. For this reason, we will view the China mainland as it is at the present time.

Eastfoto/Hsiao Chua

The Yangtze Kiang, which rises in the high mountains of Tibet and flows across China to the sea, is the country's largest river. Trace its course on the map on page 30. Thousands of boats, like those shown in the picture, carry passengers and goods to the great cities far up the river.

Chinese People

CHINA'S THREE REGIONS

Geographers usually divide the mainland of China into three regions. The regions are South China and North China, divided by the **Tsinling** \\'jin-'ling\\ **Mountains,** and Outer China, which lies to the north and west.

The Green South

If you lived in South China, the landscape around you would be green all year long. Everywhere you looked, you would see rice growing in flooded fields and hilltops covered with bamboo. Ponds and streams would glint in the warm sun. The banks of the many canals would be lined with willows and mulberry trees.

The rainfall in South China is about 55 inches a year. The rains come all through the year, but summer rains are heavier than winter ones.

In summer, especially in the lowlands, the temperature often rises to 90° F. In winter it seldom goes as low as 50° F. Because the growing season is ten months' long, farmers can plant and harvest two crops a year.

Winds and mountains have much to do with South China's weather. The winds are called **monsoons** \män-'sünz\ because they change direction with the change of the seasons. They blow in one direction in summer and in the opposite direction in winter. Monsoon means "season."

In summer the monsoons blow from the Pacific and Indian oceans over the continent of Asia. Air that blows in from the sea carries a great deal of moisture. As the summer monsoons blow across the hills of South China, they drop their moisture in the form of rain.

In winter the monsoons blow from the center of Asia out to sea. Air that blows from the interior of a continent is cold and dry. The winter monsoons bring freezing temperatures. Then why doesn't South China have cold weather in winter? Because the winter monsoons never reach South China. They are blocked by the Tsinling Mountains.

Because of the warm climate and abundant rainfall, crops grow well in South China. The food produced there

Chinese Information Service

Rice is the basic food of the people of South China. Because there is not enough flat land to grow the amount of rice needed, the Chinese have dug terraces out of the mountainsides. Such terraces, shown above, are like wide level steps which become tiny farms when planted in rice.

supports many people. South China is the most crowded of China's three regions. It has most of the nation's large cities. Their narrow streets and busy marketplaces are bursting with people. There, too, farmers make the fullest use of land. Since South China has many hills and mountains, flat land—where farming is easiest—is scarce. The Chinese have met this problem by digging **terraces,** or steps, up the hillsides and mountain slopes. These terraces provide level plots where crops are grown. Many hillsides and mountain slopes in South China have such terraces going almost to their tops.

Except in the cities, houses in South China today are like the houses people lived in 2,500 years ago. They are usually made either of mud bricks or of woven bamboo. Because of the warm climate they do not need to be heated. People wear just one layer of clothing, usually made of cotton. Some people wear silk clothes on special occasions.

33

Eastfoto

In North China the basic grain of the people is wheat. The Loess Highlands and the North China Plain produce much wheat. Above we see a bumper crop being harvested. Wheat was grown very early in North China.

The Brown North

The eastern part of North China is made up mostly of two broad plains. These plains are brown and dusty except during part of the spring and summer, when growing crops turn the landscape green. People do their traveling on narrow dirt roads instead of in boats on canals as in the south. Unlike the canals the roads are seldom lined with trees. The main crop in North China is not rice but wheat. The growing season is four to six months long, and farmers grow one crop a year.

The western part of North China contains many mountains and hills. In this area are the **Loess** \les\ **Highlands,** where Chinese civilization began. The highlands get their name from the fine, soft, yellow soil called loess that covers them. Geographers believe that winds brought the loess, or "loose" soil, from deserts far to the north and west. The deposits of loess in the highlands are 50 to 300 feet thick.

Summers in North China are short, hot, and rainy. The temperature sometimes rises to 100° F. The rainfall is about

20 inches a year, just enough for most crops. Winters in this region are long, cold, and dry. The temperature usually falls far below zero.

North China's climate is greatly influenced by the monsoons. The summer monsoons blow in from the sea and bring the rain. The winter monsoons blow out from the interior of Asia and bring the bitter cold.

Except in the cities the houses of North China today are like those that people inhabited 2,500 years ago. Some people live in caves dug out of the hillsides. Others live in houses made of packed earth or sundried brick.

In winter people in North China must wear several layers of clothing to protect themselves against the cold and the wind. They often describe the weather according to the number of layers of clothing needed. A nine-layer day is bitterly cold. A three-layer day is merely chilly.

In summer people look as if they have been on a reducing diet. Off come the heavy clothes and padded jackets. They are replaced by a single layer of cotton clothing. Now you can tell what size a person really is.

Outer China

Outer China has three sections. From north to south, the sections are Inner Mongolia, **Sinkiang** \'shin-jē-äng\, and **Tibet** \tə'bet\. You will find these sections on the map on page 30.

The land in Outer China consists of mountain ranges and flat highlands. In winter the temperature falls far below zero. In summer the temperature varies. In some places it is always cool. In other places it is warm during the day but cool at night.

Because Outer China is so far from the ocean, the average rainfall is less than 10 inches a year. Much of the land is desert. The Gobi is one of the largest deserts in the world. It lies partly in Inner Mongolia and partly in the neighboring nation of the Mongolian People's Republic.

Some parts of Outer China receive from 10 to 20 inches of rain. In these areas short grass grows, and herds of animals graze there.

In other parts of Outer China streams and wells are fed by melting snow from the mountains. In such areas the land can be farmed. People live in villages. The farmers go out each day to their farms and return at night. But in most places lack of water makes raising crops impossible. In the areas where the short grass grows the people move from place to place in search of fresh pastures for their sheep. These nomads use either horses or two-humped camels to carry their possessions. From their sheep they get mutton for food, sheepskins for clothing, dung for fuel, and wool for tents.

In Sinkiang, in Outer China, many people are nomads who travel about to find grass for their sheep. They live in tents made of wool. Find Sinkiang on the map on page 30. Why does Sinkiang receive so little rain?

U.P.I. Photo

CHINA'S WATERWAYS

China's rivers, especially the Yangtze Kiang and the Hwang Ho, have played a large part in the lives of the people. In ancient times the Chinese believed that their rivers were controlled by a spirit called the Dragon King. Usually the Dragon King was good. Year after year he kept the rivers filled with water so that the farmers could irrigate their fields. Sometimes, however, the Dragon King became angry. Then he would blow away the clouds so that no rain fell. Or he would use his tail to lash the rivers until they leaped over their banks and overflowed the land.

The Yangtze Kiang: "Main Street" of China

The Yangtze rises in northern Tibet, more than 3,400 miles from the Pacific Ocean into which it finally empties. For almost half its length it is a wild river flowing between canyons that tower more than a mile above it. It whirls over rocky ledges and plunges with a roar to the plain below.

About halfway between its source and its mouth the Yangtze leaves the highlands of Tibet and enters an area known as the Red Basin. The basin really *is* red. The mountains surrounding it are red sandstone, and the fertile soil covering its hilly floor is also red. From the Red Basin on the river is wide enough for ships to sail all the way to the ocean.

The river flows quietly through the Red Basin until it reaches Chungking at the eastern end of the basin. Chungking is the market center of the basin area. Farmers bring their goods here and load them on steamers and **junks,** or large sailing ships, for the long journey downstream.

From Chungking on, the Yangtze deserves its title of China's "Main Street." It serves as a water roadway through

Eastfoto

As the Yangtze Kiang cuts its way through the mountains of central China, it flows between high cliffs, or gorges. Why are few boats seen in the gorge section of the Yangtze? Between what cities is the gorge section found?

the heart of China. The country has few railroads or highways. There is little gasoline for trucks and almost no cargo planes. As a result, the best way to move goods in China is by water. The Yangtze carries about half of all the goods that move through China.

About 350 miles downstream from Chungking is the city of **Ichang** \ 'ē-'chäng\. The part of the river between these two cities is called the **gorge** \'görj\ **section** because of the sheer cliffs that rise on either side. This gorge section is very beautiful but it is the most difficult part of the Yangtze for boats. Whirlpools, rocks hidden below the river's surface, and sudden stretches of shallow water challenge the great skill of the Chinese boatmen.

Beyond Ichang, the Yangtze flows more slowly and becomes almost a mile wide. The next major city downstream is **Wuhan** \'wü-hän\. Wuhan stands at the spot where the Yangtze is joined by the Han River, its largest tributary. Actually, Wuhan is a group of three cities. One is a banking center. Another is a textile center. And the third is an iron-and-steel center. The only railroad line between North and South China crosses the Yangtze on the Wuhan bridge.

From Wuhan to the sea the Yangtze is jammed with all sorts of vessels. There are large ocean-going freighters. There are junks and river steamers. There are timber rafts as large as a baseball diamond. There are small, flat-bottomed **sampans** \'sam-'panz\ which have tiny cabins made of bamboo mats. There are fishing boats just long enough for a man to lie down in and houseboats big enough to sleep twenty persons. In some places along the Yangtze whole villages are made up of moored houseboats. Many families spend their entire lives on the water. Harbors and riverfronts are jammed with boats that serve people as homes.

The Yangtze widens still more as it nears the Pacific. A person standing on one bank can scarcely see the opposite bank two miles away. Also, the ocean tides sweep 200 miles up the river, past the city of Nanking.

Most of the land between Nanking and the sea is a **delta,** or soil deposited by the river at its mouth. Each year the

In various countries of Southeast Asia, people make their homes on houseboats, called sampans. Usually sampans anchor at the water front, but here some are parked on Main Street. Note the bamboo mats on the cabins.

U.P.I. Photo

Yangtze carries millions of tons of yellow mud down from South China's hills and mountains. It drops its load along the shore. The land increases in height about one foot every 20 years. Every 60 to 70 years the delta extends one mile farther into the sea.

The delta of the Yangtze is crossed by small canals that join one village to another. Small boats go from village to village, carrying passengers and cargo. The canals have bridges that curve high in the middle so that vessels can sail under them.

The Chinese who live in the Yangtze delta use the canals for more than transportation. They get their household water from the canals. They wash their clothing in them and fish for food there. They let their work animals, the water buffaloes, soak in the canals to prevent the animals' skins from cracking in the hot sun. And they dump their garbage into the canals. Do you wonder why the Chinese drink tea rather than water? Drinking unboiled water would make them sick!

The cargo that moves downstream along the Yangtze finally reaches the great port of **Shanghai** \shang-'hī\. Shanghai does not lie at the mouth of the river itself. Rather, it is on a tributary 13 miles from the river's mouth. The reason for this is that the mouth of the Yangtze does not have a harbor where ships can anchor. Also, the river's mouth is shallow and filled with sandbars through which large ships cannot move.

Although built on mud flats, Shanghai has many skyscrapers. Its growing population now numbers 10,000,000, making it the second largest city in the world. In addition to being China's biggest port, it is the nation's leading industrial center.

The Hwang Ho: "China's Sorrow"

The course of the Hwang Ho, or Yellow River, resembles that of the Yangtze. Both rivers rise in Tibet and empty into the Pacific Ocean. Both rivers begin as clear tumbling streams flowing through a deep canyon. Both rivers drop from the Tibet highlands, pass slowly through an open valley, flow swiftly through a gorge section, then enter a great plain. In both cases much of the plain has been built by the river as it drops mud year after year.

Unlike the Yangtze, the Hwang Ho is almost useless for transportation. Ships cannot sail on it. Either it flows too swiftly, or there are too many waterfalls, or it is too shallow. However, the river is the farmers' friend. Since rainfall is light throughout much of North China, farmers depend on water from the Hwang River system to irrigate their crops.

Yet the Chinese call the Hwang Ho "China's Sorrow." To understand why, you must know something about the river's behavior as it flows across the Yellow Plain.

A person who looks down from a plane at the Pacific Ocean about 100 miles east of the Hwang's mouth sees water that is yellow. The water is yellow because of the mud the Hwang Ho dumps into the ocean. Each year vast quantities of yellow earth slide down the hills and into the river. The river in turn either deposits the mud on the Yellow Plain or dumps it into the Pacific Ocean.

All large rivers, of course, carry mud to the sea. Many build up deltas at their mouths. What is different about the Hwang Ho?

One difference is the amount of mud carried by the Hwang Ho. Mud makes up 10 to 40 per cent of the weight of the Hwang's water. Most large rivers carry only 2 to 3 per cent of their weight in mud.

The other difference is that the Hwang cannot now deposit its mud on the plain. Tens of thousands of years ago, before men lived in the Yellow Plain, the Hwang Ho flowed where it pleased. It dropped its mud gradually over a large area. After it built up the land to a certain height, it left its channel and found a new exit to the sea on lower ground. Then it would build up the lower ground and change its course again.

The early Chinese on the Yellow Plain found it difficult to live in an area where the river kept changing its course. So they built dikes of earth, one on each side of the river, to keep the Hwang Ho in place. Building these dikes solved one problem for the farmers. But it created another problem for them.

The Hwang Ho was no longer able to spread its load of mud in a thin layer over a large area. Instead, it spread its mud in a thick layer over a narrow area. This raised the river bed so that when a great flood came the river flowed over the dikes and across the farmers' fields. The farmers built the dikes higher. After a while the river again raised its bed and overflowed. The farmers built the dikes higher still. And so it went, on and on and on, through the centuries. Today the river flows from 10 to 40 feet above the land outside the dikes.

Another problem arises when the Hwang Ho breaks *through* the dikes in one spot or another as it does about every second year. Because the river flows on a ridge, the water cannot drain back. Instead it remains on the land until it evaporates. This sometimes takes as long as three years. So in addition to destroying growing crops, a Hwang flood prevents farmers from planting new crops. Is it any wonder that the river is known as "China's Sorrow"?

Eastfoto

The Grand Canal, once called the "grain transport river," is about 1,100 miles long. It is the world's longest canal. In this picture we see boats passing through the gates of one of the locks. Locks are used at points where boats must be raised or lowered as the water level changes.

The Grand Canal

Both the Yangtze Kiang and the Hwang Ho flow generally in a west-to-east direction. To help traffic move north and south, the Chinese built a waterway to link their two main rivers. They called this man-made waterway the Grand Canal. It is about 1,100 miles long. This makes it one of the longest man-made waterways in the world.

The Grand Canal was built entirely by human labor. Most of the work was done during the Sui Dynasty, which ended in 618 A.D. Estimates of the number of workmen vary, but most historians agree that the emperor drafted at least 1,000,000 men a year for six years.

In addition to digging the canal itself, the workers built a road on each bank and set out trees along the roads. They also built 40 palaces along the canal. Each palace was a day's sail away from the next palace. This made it easy for the emperor to travel through the country in style and comfort.

The Grand Canal helped to keep the farmers of the Yellow Plain from starving. If floods or drought destroyed their crops, the government could ship rice to them from South China. The canal was also useful to merchants who wanted to avoid sea pirates who roamed along the coast.

VILLAGES AND CITIES

About 90 per cent of the Chinese people—or about 675,000,000 persons—live in villages. There are about 600,000 villages on the China mainland. They range in size from a few hundred inhabitants to a few thousand.

About 10 per cent of the Chinese people—or about 75,000,000 persons—live in cities. Most live in medium-sized cities, that is, cities whose population ranges from 50,000 to 500,000.

Some Chinese, however, live in very large cities. Shanghai's population numbers 10,000,000. Peking, the capital, has a population of about 6,000,000. Eighteen other cities have more than 1,000,000 inhabitants each. Among these cities are Chungking, Wuhan, and Canton in South China and **Tientsin** \tē'ent-'sin\ and Mukden in North China.

When most of China's cities were first built, they were surrounded by walls. Through the years towns grew up along the main roads that led into the city from the surrounding countryside. In recent years the Chinese have knocked down the walls in order to build wide avenues in their place. A city and its nearby towns, or suburbs, now join one another without interruption.

I. Word Study

Match each word in **Column 1** with its meaning in **Column 2.**

Column 1   **Column 2.**

1. delta   a. A ship with a large bamboo sail
2. gorge   b. A boat with a cabin made of bamboo mats
3. junk   c. A narrow river valley with steep walls
4. loess   d. Soil deposited at a river's mouth
5. monsoon   e. Fine, yellow soil deposited by wind
6. sampan   f. A wide step cut into a hillside
7. terrace   g. A seasonal wind

II. Reviewing What You Have Learned

Make three columns on your paper under the headings: **South China, North China,** and **Outer China.** Put each of these activities under its proper heading.

   a. Farmers harvesting wheat
   b. People harvesting rice
   c. Farmers working in rice paddies
   d. People living in caves dug out of loess
   e. Farmers weeding fields in October
   f. Nomads with flocks of sheep
   g. Ocean-going freighters moving up a river
   h. Bamboo growing in forests
   i. People wearing padded jackets
   j. Water buffalo pulling plows
   k. People sleeping on heated brick shelves
   l. A dust storm

III. Can You Explain?

1. Why the Yangtze Kiang is called "China's Main Street."
2. Why the Hwang Ho is called "China's Sorrow."

Courtesy Art Institute of Chicago
Lucy Maud Buckingham Collection

The swans shown above were made of bronze. Bronze art work developed early in China. The painted paper scroll, at the left, is a fine specimen of the landscape art of Old China.

Courtesy Art Institute of Chicago
Kate S. Buckingham Fund

UNIT 3

The Arts

What was it that held the Chinese people together during thousands of years of history and over such a large expanse of land? The family system, as we have learned, was one important factor. Another was the writing system, which was in use as early as the time of the Shang dynasty. And a third factor was the system of government.

Amer. Mus. Hist.

Eastfoto

Fine brush writing, which is an art in China, developed into painting. This Chinese man is writing lucky New Year mottoes on a red paper scroll.

of Civilization

WRITING AND RULING

The original language of the Chinese was Mandarin. As the people spread out over the land and formed new communities, the language changed. In some places it changed so much that it became a different language, or **dialect.**

The most common Chinese dialect is Cantonese, which is spoken by most of the Chinese who live in the United States. There are five or six other important dialects, each spoken by several million people. Most of the people on the China mainland, however, speak Mandarin.

Mandarin is very different from English. Instead of combining sounds to make words, Mandarin combines syllables to make words. However, there are only 400 or so syllables with which to make tens of thousands of words. As a result, each syllable must do duty for a number of words.

To solve this problem, the Chinese use different tones of voice to convey their meaning. When a speaker pronounces a syllable using a high pitch, it has a different meaning than when pronounced at a low pitch.

The Chinese Writing System

Because the same syllable has several different meanings, the Chinese developed a pictorial kind of writing rather than an alphabet as we did. A written word in Chinese does not consist of letters. It consists of a character or a group of characters.

Characters in Chinese writing work something like symbols for numbers do. When a Frenchman and Englishman write "2," they write it the same way. The Frenchman calls this symbol "deux." The Englishman calls it "two." But both use the symbol "2" in writing and give it the same meaning. That is just the way Chinese writing works. A character may be pronounced one way in Mandarin and another way in Cantonese. But it looks the same when written and means the same. So you can see how the writing system helped to hold the Chinese people together.

Chinese writing is difficult to learn. A person who wants to read a newspaper must memorize about 1,000 different characters. If he wants to read a book, he must memorize more than 2,500 characters. And if he goes to college, he probably needs to know about 10,000 characters.

The Chinese government recently tried to make writing easier by adopting an alphabet very similar to the one we use. Street signs in the largest cities are now written in both the old characters and the new alphabet. But the government has not required everyone to learn the new alphabet. If it did, after awhile no one would know how to read the great works of the past.

THE TWO THOUSAND YEAR GOVERNMENT

Another important aid to Chinese unity was the pattern of government. It was based in part on Confucius's idea that government officials should be well-educated and chosen by examination. Every boy might aspire to take the **civil-service** examinations which would qualify him to become a public official. Usually, though, only the sons of gentry families could afford the years of schooling. Also, the tests were difficult and only a few could pass them all.

The Great Examination

Cheng She Kit sat in the great examination hall, waiting for the examination to begin. He kept rubbing his perspiring hands on his thick cotton pants.

"Funny that I am so nervous for this examination," he thought. "My mouth is so dry I can barely swallow, and my tongue feels as big as a melon."

Cheng She Kit had already passed two examinations, one in his county and one in his state. Now the three days of the national examination lay ahead.

She Kit remembered how proud the whole Cheng family had been when he passed the county examination. His father had said, "Well done, my son." And his stern grandfather had waggled his white beard to show his pleasure.

The entire village had rejoiced when he passed the state examination. "You will surely become a **chin-shih** \\'jin-'shir\\, a scholar who has passed the national examination," the rich Mr. Wu had said. He had given She Kit a new set of writing brushes and a hard stick of black ink to use when taking the national examination.

She Kit was thinking about all this when he saw the examiner walking to the center of the raised platform at the front of the hall. Quickly he cut a piece from the stick of ink and began mixing it with the water on his palette. The ink was ready when the examiner began to read.

He read a passage from the teachings of Confucius. As he read, She Kit wrote down the words, painting each character as beautifully as he could. Then he wrote an explanation of what the words meant. The examiner read another passage. She Kit wrote down the words and his explanation. This continued all that day, and the next, and the next.

By the end of the third day She Kit's head was swimming. His back ached, and his fingers were stiff from holding the writing brush. He was glad the examination was over. But it would be a week before the results were announced.

"At least I know that the examiner will be fair in marking the tests," he thought. He remembered that three years ago, during the last national examination, an examiner had been caught giving an extra high mark to his first cousin. The government officials had thrown the candidate out and forbade him ever to take another examination. As for the examiner, they had paraded him in disgrace through the streets of the capital. Then they had cut off his head!

At last the week of waiting was over. Once again She Kit sat in the great examination hall, rubbing his hands on his thick cotton pants. Once again the examiner walked to the center of the platform at the front of the hall. With great dignity he began to read the names of the successful candidates.

"Chao Han-min. Chen Hsun. Cheng She Kit. . . ."

She Kit stopped listening when he heard his name. It was true. He had passed. He was really a chin-shih. Already he could see himself governing a county somewhere in China. His name would be engraved on a stone tablet in the capital. His family would be honored for having produced a scholar. And his village would honor his name long after his death.

The Chinese Civil Service

In one way, the county, state, and national examinations that Cheng She Kit passed were like federal civil-service examinations in the United States. The purpose of the examinations was to select qualified people to work in the government.

What made a person qualified to rule in Old China? It was not having a special skill, for the Chinese believed that a man could always learn a job while doing it. The important thing was for a man to be well-educated. In Old China this meant knowing the teachings of Confucius and other wise men of China by heart.

China established its civil-service system about 124 B.C., during the Han dynasty. With a few changes, the system worked for almost 2,000 years. Its officers, or chin-shih, were usually among the more intelligent and able people in the nation. They all received the same kind of education. They held the same ideas about the importance of loyalty to their superiors. And they usually applied the laws in the same manner. This system of government helped to unify the Chinese people.

Local Government

The chin-shih were concerned mostly with such matters as collecting taxes and drafting young men into the army. Other government matters were usually left to the people.

For example, suppose a man were accused of stealing another man's plow. If this occurred in the United States, the two men would appear before a judge in a local court. In Old China the matter was usually settled by the heads of the two families. They would meet to decide whether or not the accused was guilty. If they found him guilty, they would also say how he should be punished. It was a rare case that had to be taken before a chin-shih because it could not be settled by family heads.

The Role of the Emperor

Confucius taught that the nation was very much like the family. The emperor was the nation's head just as the father was the family's head. The father's duty was to care for his children. The emperor's duty was to care for his subjects. Children were supposed to be obedient and respectful toward their father. And people were supposed to be obedient and respectful toward the emperor.

According to Confucius a good emperor was one who behaved properly and thus set an example for his people to follow. When Confucius was once asked by a lord how to rule, he answered:

"To govern is to keep straight. If you, Sir, lead the people straight, which of your subjects will venture to fall out of line?"

The emperor made all the laws of the land. The laws were carried out by the chin-shih.

The emperor also performed certain religious ceremonies. He welcomed the four seasons of the year at the gates of his capital city. He greeted spring at the east gate, summer at

Amer. Mus. Nat. Hist.

This gate in Peking is an example of the old Chinese art of stone carving. The architecture of ancient China, especially the temples and pavilions, featured upward-curving roofs like those around the lookout tower here.

the south gate, autumn at the west gate, and winter at the north gate. Each spring, when the ground was frost-free, he plowed three furrows in a special field as an example to the nation's farmers. On the longest night of the year he made offerings to heaven. On the longest day of the year he made offerings to the earth.

The Chinese believed that the gods gave the emperor the right to rule. They called this the **"mandate** \\'man-,dāt\\ **of Heaven."** The emperor kept the mandate, or command of the gods, as long as he behaved properly and performed his duties. However, if he were dishonest, or if he allowed war and misery to spread through the land, he lost his "mandate." Then the people had the right to rebel against him and place a different emperor on the throne.

CHINESE ART

We have seen some of the things that helped to hold the Chinese people together on their "Long March" through history. Now we will look at some of the gifts the Chinese made to the world.

Confucius believed that the most admirable thing about a nation is the art its people produce. Painting, literature, and music, he said, make life good and show the real difference between one nation and another. The people of Old China produced many beautiful works of art.

The Horses of T'ang

The Chinese developed early the useful skill of making vessels from clay. Over the years they made other **ceramics** \sə-'ram-iks\, or pottery objects. Among the most beautiful are figures of horses, made during the T'ang dynasty which ruled China from 618 A.D. to 907 A.D. Art museums that possess any of these horses consider them among their finest treasures. Powerful yet graceful, the horses seem to be almost alive.

Ceramic horses became popular during the T'ang dynasty for an unusual reason. In those days a man would order a coffin as soon as he owned a house. A government official

The early Chinese excelled in the art of making pottery, or ceramics. Ceramic horses were valued by the T'ang rulers. This one is so real, it was probably modeled from life. The kneeling ram, shown below, is made of bronze and dates from the Han dynasty. It served as a lamp, when oil was burned in it.

Photos Courtesy The Asia Society

Collection of Dr. Paul Singer

Avery Brundage Collection

would build a tomb and furnish it with figures of servants made from clay. The figures were hardened and glazed by skilled craftsmen.

The second T'ang emperor was extremely fond of horses. He owned eight magnificent steeds that went with him into battle. The story is told that the steeds once saved his life by blocking enemy arrows with their own bodies. In any event, the emperor decided to furnish his tomb with ceramic figures of his eight steeds. No sooner had he done so than all the members of his court decided to follow his example.

China and Jade

The Chinese made porcelain as well as pottery from clay. Porcelain is made from a special kind of clay that is baked at great heat. Fine porcelain has a very smooth surface and is so thin that light will show through. Beginning with the Han dynasty, the Chinese made beautiful porcelain cups, saucers, plates, and vases. This porcelain ware became one of China's major exports. Europeans called it chinaware, or simply china.

At first the porcelain was white, but after a time Chinese pottery makers learned how to give it a colored coating, or glaze. In the beginning the glazes were usually a rich brown or a beautiful green—the color of sea water. Later, as many as five colors were used at a time. The most popular combination was blue and white.

Expert Chinese craftsmen also learned to make designs on porcelain. Pictures of dragons with long tails curved around the edge of a bowl. Willow trees bent over the sides of a cup. Men and women were shown walking through a garden or across a bridge in the center of a plate.

Chinese craftsmen turned out other beautiful objects. Among the materials they liked best to use, especially for

Avery Brundage Collection
Photos Courtesy The Asia Society

The fine pottery called porcelain was first made in China. This porcelain jar has a design of fish and flowers. The pig shown above was carved from the semiprecious stone called jade. How was jade carved?

jewelry, was **jade** \ˈjād\. Jade is a stone that comes in many colors, including green, yellow, red, violet, black, and white. It is harder than steel. It took Chinese craftsmen long hours to polish away the roughness of the stone and to drill and carve the fine designs.

Painting

Chinese painting developed out of the Chinese writing system. Scribes formed characters with graceful strokes of brush and ink. After a time, they began using the same method to draw pictures. The pictures were painted on either paper or silk. The most beautiful pictures were done during the T'ang and Sung dynasties.

Chinese artists liked to draw human figures and animals, but their favorite subject was landscapes. The word for landscape in Mandarin is **shan-shui** \ˈshän-ˈshü-ē\, meaning "mountain and water." Most Chinese landscapes pictured a mountain and a body of water. The reason was that the earliest inhabitants of the Yellow Plain regarded mountains and rivers as sacred. Mountains surrounded the Yellow Plain and protected it, while rivers brought needed water to the fields.

Chinese artists liked color but they did not consider it important. They did many paintings in different shades of a single color. What *was* important to the Chinese was the spirit of the thing that was being painted. In painting a willow, for example, the artist tried to bring out its gentleness and grace. In painting a pine tree, he tried to show its dignity.

Poetry

From early times the Chinese have respected writing and admired writers, especially people who composed poems. Like painting, writing poetry reached its peak during the T'ang and Sung dynasties.

It is not possible to enjoy a Chinese poem fully if it is translated into English because the beauty of the sounds is lost. However, a good translation helps the reader to understand the feelings of the poet and his message.

Here are two poems from Old China translated into English. The first describes a scene at a farm house.

"Our little servant is tying the feet of a chicken which he is going to carry to the market. The chicken flutters and cries.

"My father looks at it without pity. My mother has turned away her head. A sparrow in the branches of the tree is frisking joyfully about, for now there will be more grain for him."

The second poem is about armies that invaded the empire and the call to battle.

"It is always in the early autumn that our enemies come down from the mountains to invade our country.

"The call to arms has sounded! Our warriors soon will cross the Great Wall and they will not stop until they have reached the Desert of Gobi.

"Out there they will see only the cold moon. Out there how they will shiver at the hour when the dew freezes on sword and armor!

"Weep not, young women! You will weep too long!"

Actors and the Theater

Chinese plays developed out of the art of storytelling. The theater began in the early days of the empire, but it did not become important until the days of the Mongols. The Mongols did not know how to read, but they enjoyed plays and supported the theater. By the end of their rule, in the middle 1300's, almost every Chinese town had a raised platform where traveling bands of actors performed.

The Chinese stage had no curtain and practically no scenery. But, oh, the costumes and the make-up! The actors, even those taking the parts of poor peasants, wore floor-length robes of silk embroidered in rich designs. Headdresses had long feathers and balls of many colors hanging from them. The color and pattern of the make-up worn by players told the audience what kind of person each actor was portraying. If his face was painted black, you knew he was cruel. If the face appeared white, he was dishonest and would undoubtedly betray his troops to the enemy. A just man was painted green. An honest man was painted red.

Chinese actors all spoke in high-pitched voices. In addition to being good actors, they had to know how to sing and to be good at gymnastics. There was always some singing in a Chinese play and usually several sword dances to show battle scenes. There was an orchestra of gongs and flutes.

This girl, heroine of the Chinese opera, wears red make up. Can you tell why? By putting her hand on her heart, she is using a gesture well known to the audience. This gesture tells them that she is doomed soon to die.

U.P.I. Photo

Most Chinese plays were short, so several were usually given on the same program. There was no intermission. As soon as one play was finished, the next play began. People in the audience would wander around the theater, talking with friends, and even eating dinner while watching the show.

In addition to being entertaining, Chinese plays taught moral lessons. They taught the importance of loyalty to the emperor and about the devotion of a son to his parents. In other words, the plays taught the Chinese way of life.

INVENTIONS AND CONSTRUCTIONS

Confucius was interested in human relationships but not at all in science. Chinese scholars did not spend much time thinking about or investigating the physical world. They discovered none of the basic laws of science.

The Chinese did, however, develop a great many practical inventions. They also performed splendid engineering feats.

Cloth From Caterpillars

In ancient times a trade route extended across Asia. It wound through barren flatlands, snow-covered mountain passes, and along the edge of a great desert. It was more than 6,000 miles long. Yet from about 200 B.C. to about 1400 A.D., a steady stream of traffic moved along this route.

Caravans \\'kar-ə-vanz\\, or long trains of pack animals, moved along the route. Donkeys traveled in the eastern part. Camels plodded through the deserts of the western part. The caravans from southern Europe to China carried mostly gold. In the opposite direction they carried mostly silk. The route was known as the Silk Road.

People in southern Europe were eager to buy silk from China. In those days, European clothes were made mostly of wool. Much of the wool cloth was rough and scratchy and came in only two or three colors. Silk, on the other hand, was soft and smooth. It came in many colors and often had beautiful raised designs woven in. Everyone who saw the shimmering fabric wanted it. Prosperous Europeans willingly paid large sums of gold to buy it.

When and how did the Chinese discover silk? We don't know for certain. But a well-known Chinese legend says it happened in this way.

More than 4,500 years ago a beautiful 14-year-old empress was sitting in the palace garden in the shade of a white mulberry tree. Having little else to do, she watched the movements of silk-moth caterpillars on the tree. Some caterpillars were feeding on the mulberry leaves. Others were spinning out yard after yard of a creamy white thread and wrapping it around their bodies.

A few days later, when the empress again entered the garden, the caterpillars had disappeared. Instead, the mulberry tree was covered with plump white cocoons that gleamed like jewels in the sun.

"Wouldn't it be wonderful to have a robe that looks like that!" the empress thought.

She picked the cocoons off the tree and carefully unwound the tiny strands of gleaming thread. She twisted the threads together into a yarn strong enough for weaving. She gathered more cocoons and made more yarn. Finally she had enough yarn to weave cloth for a robe for her husband, the emperor. From that time on, say the Chinese, the ladies of the court spent most of their time raising silk-moth caterpillars and making silk.

At first silk was used only for robes worn by the emperor and people at his court. Then the Chinese began to use the material in other ways. They decorated their temples with

Amer. Mus. Nat. Hist.

In ancient times long camel trains like this followed the Silk Route, carrying products between India and China. What were the main articles traded?

silk banners. They wrote poems on silk scrolls and painted pictures on silk hangings. And caravans carried loads of silk over the Silk Route to exchange for gold.

Silk making became one of Old China's most important industries. The Chinese kept the ways of making silk a secret for several thousand years. Sometime after 100 A.D., however, Buddhist monks carried the knowledge with them to Korea. From there it spread to Japan, which is now the world's largest silk-producing nation. In the next century a Chinese princess, going to India to marry an Indian prince, hid some silk-moth eggs among her wedding things. She wanted to continue to wear silk. In India people began to raise silk worms and to produce silk. From India silk making spread to southwest Asia and later to Europe and America.

Paper and Printing

The Chinese gave the world a still more important gift than silk. They were the first people to make paper. If all the silk in the world were destroyed, life would go on as usual. But if suddenly there was no more paper in the world, life would be very different indeed.

Paper was invented in China about the year 105 A.D., during the Han dynasty. The inventor was an official named **Ts'ai Lun** \ˈtsī ˈlün\. In those days the Chinese wrote on either silk or bamboo. Silk was expensive, however, while bamboo was heavy and awkward to carry about. Tsai Lun began to experiment to find a better writing material. After a few years he was successful. He used some bark from the mulberry tree, some hemp, a few rags, and an old fishnet. He shredded these materials into bits, added water, and mashed everything together into a soggy pulp. Then he squeezed out the water until the pulp was a thin, damp sheet and hung it up to dry. This dried sheet was the world's first paper.

About four or five hundred years after the invention of paper, the Chinese invented printing. The oldest-known printed book in the world, a sacred writing of Buddhism, was printed in 868 A.D. It looks something like a thin roll of wallpaper and was made by pasting together seven separate printed sheets. At the end of the roll is the statement: "Printed . . . by Wang Jye, for free general distribution, in order in deep reverence to perpetuate [keep alive] the memory of his parents."

Printing probably grew out of the practice of writing **charms,** or magical sayings. The Chinese believed that you

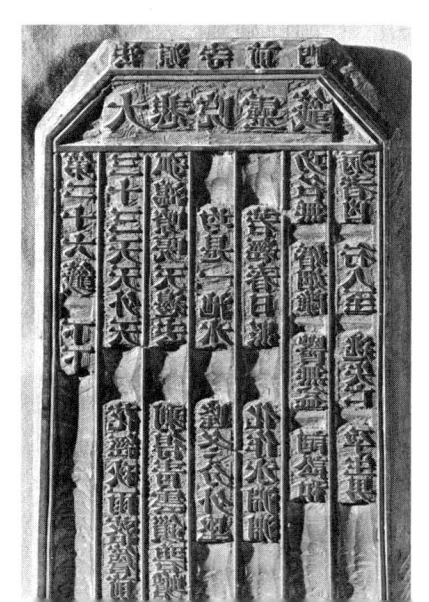

Amer. Mus. Nat. Hist.

The ancient Chinese did most of their printing from carved blocks of wood like this. The characters made a raised design. When the block was inked and pressed against another surface, a copy of the characters was left behind. A carved block of this kind was used to print one book page.

could keep away illness and misfortune if you carried a charm with you at all times. At first they stamped charms on clay with a wood seal. Then they began to ink the wood and stamp the charms on paper. The next step was printing the entire page of a book from a carved wood block.

From the T'ang dynasty on, block printing was widespread in China. The most commonly printed books were the writings of Confucius. Other books included histories and encyclopedias. Some of these books were extremely long, with as many as 5,000 chapters. It often took several generations of scholars to finish printing such a work.

The Chinese also invented **movable type** about 400 years before Europeans invented it on their own. Movable type means that each character is made separately. The characters are put together to form sentences to print a page. After each page has been printed the required number of times, the characters are separated and kept apart until they are needed on another page. The Chinese made movable type out of such materials as copper, porcelain, and wood. Because of their writing system, however, they usually preferred to print their books page by page.

Big Bangs

Have you ever watched a fireworks display and heard people say "ooh" and "aah" as great bursts of color brighten the sky? If so, you may be interested to learn that gunpowder, used in fireworks, was invented in China about 800 years ago.

The Chinese also used gunpowder in two weapons known as "heaven-shaking thunder" and "arrow of flying fire." The "heaven-shaking thunder" was something like a hand grenade. It was a bamboo container filled with gunpowder. A Chinese soldier would light the powder and then hurl the container toward the enemy. The "arrow of flying fire" was what we call a Roman candle or a rocket. It was a long tube

63

Sawders from Cushing

Chinese bridges were built with high arches to let ships with sails go under them. This is the Marble Arch bridge in Peking, a fine example of Chinese art.

of bamboo full of gunpowder. When lit at the end, the tube would fly in the opposite direction, throwing off fire and smoke. This weapon was especially useful against soldiers on horseback, since its whistling noise usually stampeded the animals.

Chinese Architecture

The Chinese have been splendid builders. Their architecture is not only designed for use but for beauty as well. Gay pavilions dot the hillsides, serving as shelters in parks and gardens. High-arched stone bridges cross the streams. Tall, slender pagodas, built as temples or memorials to honor the dead, rise against the sky. These eight-sided buildings have many stories whose upturned eaves often have bells tinkling from them.

The Great Wall

If you look back at the poem about war quoted on page 57, you will find words about warriors crossing the Great Wall. The Great Wall of China is one of the most remarkable engineering feats man has ever accomplished.

Most of the Great Wall was built in the reign of Shih Huang Ti. When he became emperor, he was concerned about protecting his nation. The biggest threat came from the nomads who lived in the rolling grasslands north of China. Shih Huang Ti decided that a wall across China's northern frontier would protect the country.

Some historians say that as many as 1,000,000 workers were drafted for the job. For seven years, winter and summer, they pounded earth, dug trenches, and baked bricks. In some places the workers had only to connect walls built earlier by small states that Shih Huang Ti had conquered. In other places the workers had to build from the beginning.

Usually workers were able to find the stone and clay they needed close at hand. Sometimes, however, no building materials were available. Then the Chinese had to bring in materials from other parts of the empire. They used a method of transportation that is still used today in China. Each worker fastened a bamboo basket to each end of a pole, filled the baskets with stone or clay, balanced the baskets across his shoulders, and walked.

China's Great Wall, which winds over plains and mountains for 2,000 miles, was built to keep out northern invaders. This picture of the wall shows it as it looked 100 years ago. It was drawn by an artist on the spot.

Charles Phelps Cushing

To feed the workers, boatloads of rice and wheat were sent as close to the northern frontier as China's waterways allowed. Then the grain was put into baskets, and the baskets were carried to the camps where the workers lived.

By the end of Shih Huang Ti's reign, the Great Wall extended a distance of about 1,400 miles (approximately the distance from New York City to Omaha). It took a man on horseback almost four weeks to ride from one end to the other.

Most of the wall was about 25 feet high and 20 feet wide. The center was made of packed earth, which was covered with brick or stone. On the top was a paved roadway protected on both sides by a **parapet** \'par-ə-,pet\, or low wall. Soldiers marched on the roadway behind the parapets. At regular intervals along the wall stood watchtowers. Here and there, the wall had gateways, or entrances, through which trading caravans could pass.

Was the Great Wall a success? Yes and no.

At times the nomads were unable to break through the wall's defenses. At other times they left their horses behind and climbed the wall with ladders. Without their horses they had to move slowly on foot and so were easily routed by Chinese soldiers.

Sometimes the nomads succeeded in bribing Chinese soldiers to let them pass through a gate. Then they would gallop through and bring havoc to the Chinese countryside. And occasionally they stormed through the wall in great numbers and conquered parts of China. The Mongols made the most successful nomad invasion in the late 1200's.

The emperors after Shih Huang Ti had the Great Wall extended westward. Later still, parts of it were rebuilt. Since then the wall has crumbled in places. But some of it still stands, more than 2,000 years after it was begun.

I. Word Study

caravan   jade   mandate of Heaven
chin-shin   movable type   civil-service examinations

Complete the sentences below by inserting the correct word or words from the list above. Do not write in this book.

1. Goods were carried by ____ on the Silk Road.
2. The ____ were good students in Old China.
3. The Chinese carved ____ into beautiful objects.
4. ____ was first used in printing by the Chinese.
5. To gain office in China people had to pass ____.
6. The Chinese believed their emperors ruled under a ____.

II. Questions for Discussion

1. In China, passing examinations was the way to qualify for office. Do you think this was a good plan? Why or why not?
2. Confucius said that a nation could be judged by the art of its people. Do you agree? If not, what is more important?

III. Things to Do

1. Suppose the officers of your town or city had to pass examinations to qualify for office. Write five questions that a candidate for mayor would have to answer satisfactorily before he could serve.
2. Pretend you are one of the workers building the Great Wall. Write a letter to your family describing your experiences.
3. Hold a Chinese exhibit in school. You might display articles made of silk, porcelain, jade, bamboo, carved wood (chopsticks, fans, and so on). Put pictures from magazines showing Chinese life on the bulletin board. Then invite another class to your exhibit and serve such Chinese products as tea and rice cakes.

UNIT 4 The Passing of Old

U.P.I. Photo

China

When Marco Polo returned home from China in 1292, he traveled by water most of the way, using the route shown on the map, page 68. He sailed in a ship like the junk shown here.

We have followed the course of China's history for almost 5,000 years from its beginnings to the middle of the Manchu dynasty in the early 1800's. We have seen the land where the Chinese people live, and we have taken a close look at early Chinese civilization. Now we shall read about Europe's challenge to China and China's response to the modern age.

THE COMING OF THE EUROPEANS

Europeans learned much about China and its advanced civilization from Marco Polo. When he returned to Venice, he told about the wonderful things he had seen. He described the silk robes worn at Kublai Khan's court. He told about black stones that gave heat when burned (we call them coal) and fleets of junks on the Yangtze and the Grand Canal.

Most Europeans thought Marco Polo had invented the stories. They called him "Marco Millions" because he talked about millions of people and millions of farms. Some Europeans, however, took him seriously. They decided it would be an excellent idea to develop trade with the little-known country of China. Since the overland journey across Asia was long, they began looking for a way to China by sea.

The Portuguese were the first to find an all-water route around Africa to India. A few years later a Portugese captain rounded southeast Asia and reached the Chinese harbor of Canton. The Portuguese made an agreement with the Chinese government, and Canton became a **treaty port,** where they traded with Chinese merchants. The British, the Dutch, and the French soon followed. They also made trade agreements with China and did business in Canton.

The Canton Trade

Until the early 1800's trade between Europe and China was limited to the treaty port of Canton. It was carried on according to rules laid down by the Chinese government. The European merchants were allowed to trade with only a few Chinese merchants. They could live only in special buildings that were put up outside the walls of Canton. And they had to pay China sums of money called **tribute.**

To the Europeans paying tribute meant paying a tax for the right to do business. The Chinese, however, looked on the paying of tribute differently. A nation that paid tribute, they believed, was acknowledging it was inferior to China.

For almost 300 years this difference in attitude had no effect on trade, so eager were the Europeans to do business with China. And no wonder. For China produced rare and lovely products that sold in Europe for many times the price the traders paid. Among the most popular products were porcelain, silk, and tea.

Wanted: More Trade

By the late 1700's the situation had changed. The Western traders were now unwilling to follow the old rules. The reason was that Europe had entered a new age. After the invention of the steam engine, steam power replaced the power of muscles, wind, and water in industry. People stopped making articles by hand at home and worked in factories in which machinery was run by steam. Hundreds of these factories sprang up, first in Great Britain and a little later in other European countries. The production of goods increased enormously. This meant that factory owners needed more and more raw materials to produce the goods and also larger markets. They naturally wanted to increase overseas trade.

But it takes two to trade, and the Chinese did not think Europe had anything worthwhile to give them. No matter what prices the European traders offered for more Chinese goods, the Manchu government turned a deaf ear.

The European traders in Canton became more and more annoyed at the Chinese. The British were probably most annoyed of all. And with reason, from their point of view. Great Britain was then the world's leading manufacturing nation. It also controlled vast territories in North America, India, Australia, and Africa. Its naval fleet was the strongest in the world, and its merchant fleet was the largest. Yet the British could trade only in Canton and were allowed to do only a limited amount of business there. Also, they had to pay tribute to the Chinese emperor for the right to trade.

Gradually the British began to break their agreement with the Chinese government. They sailed north along the coast of China, seeking new trading centers. When they reached Shanghai, they knew their search was over. For Shanghai, at the mouth of the Yangtze River, was the entrance to the entire Yangtze Valley. And in this populous area the finest silks, the best-tasting tea, and the most beautiful porcelain in China were produced. The only problem for the British was how to gain a foothold there.

THE DECLINE OF THE MANCHUS

The Europeans were becoming more and more determined to increase their trade with China. At the same time the Manchu government was becoming less and less able to resist their advances.

In 1650 China's population numbered about 150,000,000 persons. By 1800 the population had exploded to about 350,000,000 persons. In spite of this gigantic growth, the government did not provide more services to the people.

No new irrigation projects were started to increase the crop land. Nor did the government draft more soldiers to protect the people. As a result, border attacks by nomads became more frequent. In some areas farmers were never certain whether they were growing crops for themselves or for roaming bandits.

China's government failed to change when conditions changed because it was too set in its ways. Have you ever heard someone say, "I've been cooking for twenty years without any complaints. Why should I change now?" Or, "I've been doing business in this way for thirty years. Why should I try anything new?" If so, you can imagine how the emperor and the chin-shih must have felt. After all, the Chinese system of government had been working successfully for 2,000 years!

China had other problems, too. Some of the Manchu emperors were poor rulers. They appointed national officials who turned out to be dishonest. Under greedy local officials, taxes soared until they amounted to 70 per cent of a farmer's crop. This left the farmer and his family too little to live on. The farmers were miserable, and several "rice rebellions" broke out against the government. The Manchu dynasty was in trouble.

The Opium War

British traders finally found a product that Chinese merchants were willing to accept in trade. The product was **opium** \\'ō-pē-əm\\, a habit-forming drug made from a plant called the opium poppy. Opium poppies grew in India. Opium reached China by means of a three-way trade arrangement. British traders brought cotton cloth made in English factories to India where they traded it for opium. Then the traders brought the opium to China, where they exchanged it for tea and silk. The tea and silk were shipped to Britain and found a ready market there. Then the three-way trade began all over again.

At first the Chinese government did not interfere with the opium trade. However, as more and more Chinese—even officials at court—began to use the drug, the government became concerned. So it declared the opium trade illegal.

But the traders paid no attention to the government's order. Many Chinese ignored the order because they no longer had real respect for the government. Chinese merchants in Canton ignored the order because they were making so much money. And Europeans ignored the order because selling opium was an easy way to expand their Chinese trade.

The Manchu emperor became alarmed. In 1839 he sent a special official to Canton with orders to stop the opium trade,

Charles Phelps Cushing

This picture of Canton, China, made in 1852, shows the city as a busy sea port, visited by many ships. Why were foreigners eager to trade with China?

no matter how. The official promptly seized all the chests of opium belonging to British traders in Canton and destroyed them.

The British responded by declaring war on China. Their ships, with blazing guns, steamed northward from Canton to Shanghai and then up the Yangtze as far as the Grand Canal. The Chinese resisted bravely. But it was a hopeless fight. Spears and bows could not compete with Western cannon, nor sailing junks with steam-driven warships.

In 1842 the Manchu government acknowledged its defeat and signed a **peace treaty** with Great Britain. The treaty gave Britain the island of Hong Kong, near Canton, and trading rights in four ports besides Canton. One of these treaty ports was Shanghai.

The treaty also gave Britain the right to do business in the Western way rather than in the Chinese way. Instead of paying tribute, British traders now paid a **tariff,** or tax.

Instead of dealing with only a few Chinese merchants, British traders were now free to do business with all. Most important, China accepted the British government as an equal.

Changes in China

With the end of the Opium War time no longer stood still in China. On the contrary. Changes followed one another like the flood waters of the Yellow River.

Perhaps the greatest change that came to China was the influence exerted by foreign businessmen. Other nations soon gained the same rights in China as Britain had. Among these nations were France, Germany, Japan, Russia, and the United States.

Sections of Canton, Shanghai, and other ports became more foreign than Chinese. Instead of living under Chinese law, Western traders in these cities obeyed their own laws. For example, if a British trader committed a crime, he was tried in a British court instead of a Chinese one.

There were several reasons why the British felt their citizens had to be protected by British law. Chinese courts did not permit an accused person to have a lawyer to defend him, while British courts insisted on a defense lawyer. The Chinese custom was to torture prisoners, but the British no longer allowed this. Of course, British law was more humane than Chinese law. But the Chinese found it humiliating not to be able to govern their own treaty ports.

The cities themselves changed greatly. Shanghai was a good example. From a medium-sized city of 300,000 inhabitants, it grew during the late 1800's into a metropolis of more than 3,000,000. Before the Opium War, it had handled only goods moving from one part of China to another. By the end of the 1800's, it was the fifth largest port in the world. Ships from many nations called there. The people of Shanghai had formerly earned their living by trading and fishing. Now

U.P.I. Photo

Many foreign nations organized trade relations with China after the Opium War and set up businesses. The American settlement in Shanghai looked like this in the early 1900's. Each foreign settlement flew its own flag.

many worked in factories built and run by the foreigners. Half of China's industry was carried on in Shanghai.

The factories had a great effect on the Chinese way of life. People could now earn a living as individuals rather than as family members. The absolute control the Chinese father had over his children began to weaken.

The Boxer Rebellion

How did the Chinese people feel about the increased importance of foreigners in their nation? They did not like it at all.

One reason was that their national pride was deeply hurt. Their civilization was an ancient one. The empire had existed for 2,000 years. The Chinese had invented, among other things, silk, paper, printing, porcelain, gunpowder, paper money, the compass, and the wheelbarrow. The Koreans and the Vietnamese had borrowed the Chinese writing system. The Japanese had copied their architecture and some of their forms of government, too. Now all this seemed worthless in the face of Western guns and modern business methods.

Another reason the Chinese disliked Westerners was the terrible working conditions in Western-owned factories. Many workers labored twelve to fourteen hours a day, seven days a week. (No one dreamed of a 40-hour week at that time!) Six-year-old children sometimes worked in factories. At the same time, Western businessmen made tremendous profits from the factories and lived in great comfort in their sections of the cities.

Western missionaries were also unpopular. They had started coming to China not long after Marco Polo's visit.

Many of the missionaries were fine people, devoted to their religion and their work. They set up schools to teach Chinese farmers how to read and write. They tried to improve medical and sanitary conditions in the villages.

Some missionaries, however, showed little respect for Chinese ways of living. They laughed at the long robes that Chinese scholars wore. They did not observe Chinese customs or holidays. They built churches and schools in locations that the Chinese thought unsuitable. And they interfered in local quarrels about land and taxes.

The Chinese dislike of foreigners grew and grew. Finally many peasants formed armed bands known as the "Righteous and Harmonious Fists," usually called "Boxers" by Westerners. Encouraged by the Manchu government, these bands swept through northern China, attacking foreign missions, schools, and houses. They killed scores of missionaries and several thousand Chinese Christians. Entering the capital of Peking, they surrounded the foreign **legations** \li-ˈgā-shənz\, or government buildings. An army made up of soldiers from eight Western nations then went into China, rescued their citizens, and put down the uprising.

THE REPUBLICAN REVOLUTION

As time passed, many Chinese slowly began to realize that some Western ways were good. They set up schools where pupils could learn about Western science and modern ways of farming. They adopted Western attitudes toward women and said that girls, as well as boys, should receive an education. They tried to persuade Chinese businessmen to establish their own factories. In this way the profits could remain in China. Chinese students went abroad to study.

Dr. Sun, Father of the Revolution

One of the new leaders who wanted to bring changes to his nation was **Sun Yat-sen** \'sün-'yät-sen\. Sun was a patriot who perhaps did more than anyone else to change China into a republic. He was born in 1866 in a village near Canton. When he was thirteen, he went to Hawaii to join his older brother. In Hawaii he studied in a mission school for three years. Back in his home village, he found himself impatient with the old beliefs and practices. He went to the British colony of Hong Kong, studied medicine, and became a doctor.

Dr. Sun's real interest, however, was in politics and in bringing Western ideas of government to his country. At the age of 27 Dr. Sun moved to North China. There, like Confucius before him, he tried to show government officials how to become better rulers. Like Confucius, he had little success. Unlike Confucius, however, Sun did not become a teacher. He decided to start a revolution and change China to a republic. So he organized a secret society, called the "Revive China Society," and made plans to overthrow the Manchu government.

Sun Yat-sen launched his first revolt against the Manchus in 1895. It failed. Most of his followers were caught and beheaded. Dr. Sun fled to Japan. There he published a magazine in which he urged the Chinese people to overthrow the

Manchus and set up a republic. Every month he and other members of the "Revive China Society" smuggled the magazine out of Japan and into China.

To carry on his work, Sun Yat-sen went abroad to raise money from **overseas Chinese.** These were people like his older brother who had left China to live and work in Europe, the United States, and Southeast Asia. Dr. Sun toured the United States and Europe, asking aid against the Manchus.

Back home his efforts were bearing fruit. In 1911, while he was in the United States, revolts broke out all through China. Early the next year a group of Chinese leaders met in Nanking, on the Yangtze River, and declared China a republic. They chose Dr. Sun as its first president. The "Revive China Society" changed from a secret society to a political party. Its new name was **Kuomintang** \'gwō-min-'dang\, or "National People's Party." Its members are called Nationalists.

A Military Leader

After a few weeks in office, Dr. Sun realized that he and his party did not have enough power to unite China and govern it. So he sent a message to **Yuan Shih-k'ai** \'yü-än-'shir-'kī\, the commander of the emperor's army. If the emperor would give up his throne, Dr. Sun said that he would

The last Manchu emperor, shown here with his wife, the empress, was a very young man when he lost his throne. In 1912 a republic was established in China.

Charles Phelps Cushing

resign as president in favor of General Yuan. In that way the country would be under one government.

General Yuan agreed. In February, 1912, the last Manchu emperor gave up his throne, and the 2,000-year-old Chinese empire came to an end. Sun Yat-sen resigned from office, and Yuan Shih-k'ai became president of the new republic.

Governing China was not easy. The country had almost no money. However, Yuan gradually built up the power of the central government and obtained a foreign loan to keep the government going. Then he showed that he was not really in sympathy with the republic. He outlawed the Kuomintang and decided to have himself proclaimed emperor. But so many people opposed him that he took the declaration back. He died very soon after this.

After Yuan's death there was no leader strong enough to hold the country together. Instead, several generals set themselves up as rulers in different parts of China. These generals, or **warlords,** were interested in power and tried to expand their influence by attacking one another. Armies tramped across China, plundering fields and villages and killing hundreds of thousands of Chinese, with no one to stop them.

The Three Principles of the People

Sun Yat-sen wanted the Chinese to enjoy three things: Nationalism, Democracy, and Livelihood.
These three things were called the "Three Principles of the People," by Dr. Sun.
Nationalism meant a completely independent China.
Democracy meant the people should govern themselves.
Livelihood meant people should earn a good living.
The Nationalists and the Communists both support these principles but disagree on how to obtain them.

Help from the Soviet Union

Sun Yat-sen was a determined man. He would not give up his dream of a united, strong, and modern China. He asked Western nations for help. Europe, however, was recovering from World War I (1914-1918) and had neither money nor advisers to spare. The United States was not willing to give him help. So Dr. Sun turned to Russia, which had just had a change of government.

In 1917 a revolution in Russia had overthrown the emperor, or tsar. After a few months, the Russian Communist party had taken over the government. It set up the Union of Soviet Socialist Republics, which is often called simply the Soviet Union.

The Soviet Union agreed to supply Dr. Sun and the Nationalists with arms and advisers. In return, Dr. Sun promised that the Nationalists would work with the Chinese Communist party, which had been formed in Shanghai in 1921.

The Russians agreed to help Sun Yat-sen for a good reason. They hoped that after the warlords were defeated and China was united under one government, the Chinese Communists could get rid of the Nationalists. Then China, like the Soviet Union, would be a Communist nation.

From 1923 to 1925 the Soviet Union supplied the Kuomintang with money, guns, and military advisers. Gradually the Nationalist army became a modern fighting force. In 1925, led by a young general named **Chiang Kai-shek** \jē-ˈäng-ˈkī-ˈshek\, the army marched north from Canton to Peking. Within three years Chiang had either conquered the major warlords or convinced them to join the Nationalist government. But Sun Yat-sen did not live to see his country united. He died in 1925.

Chinese Information Service

Sun Yat-sen, shown above, was the leader of the revolution against the Manchus and father of the republic. Chiang Kai-shek, left, followed Dr. Sun as head of the new Chinese republic.

Chiang Kai-shek in Command

As Chiang Kai-shek's military power grew, so did his political power. By 1927 he was China's most important leader.

One of Chiang's first acts was to do to the Communists what they had planned to do to the Nationalists. He turned them out of the Kuomintang. They were bandits and traitors, he declared, and he ordered his soldiers to attack them.

The Communists fled to a hilly area in South China. The Nationalists, however, continued their attacks. So in 1934 the Communists set out for northern China, where they would be safe from Chiang's soldiers. There they waited for their chance to obtain control of the government.

In the meantime Chiang and the Nationalists had unified the coastal areas where most of the people lived. They began modernizing China. They built railroads to connect port cities. They encouraged Chinese businessmen to develop mines and factories. They sent their best college students abroad to study.

What the Nationalists did helped the city dwellers, but village life hardly changed at all. Rents and taxes were extremely high, taking most of what the peasants could make. Floods and droughts still destroyed crops and took lives. Growing enough food was as hard as ever.

No one knows what Chiang Kai-shek and the Nationalists might have accomplished if they had had time. Instead, once again, foreigners brought war to China.

War With Japan

In 1931 Japan's armies seized China's northeast province of Manchuria. Six years later, in 1937, Japan decided to try to take all of China. Its troops poured from Manchuria into the Yellow Plain. Other Japanese troops went ashore from ships at Shanghai.

The Chinese fought courageously, but their weapons were no match for those of Japan. Japanese forces gradually pushed Chinese soldiers out of the coastal area into the interior. Japanese planes bombed Chinese cities to the ground, killing millions of people. They moved toward Nanking.

In 1938 Chiang Kai-shek moved his government far inland, all the way to Chungking, 1400 miles up the Yangtze River. Millions of Chinese refugees followed him westward. Workers carried factory equipment on their backs. Students carried books and papers. Women carried babies and some household goods. They built new factories, schools, and houses around Chungking and continued resisting the enemy.

While the Nationalists were holding out against the Japanese in South China, the Communists were doing the same in North China. The Communists did not attack Japanese troops in regular battle. Instead, they used a fighting method called **guerrilla** \gə-'ril-ə\ **warfare**. They would dynamite a bridge here, blow up a fort there, and then scatter into the countryside to hide among the farmers.

JAPANESE OCCUPIED AREA IN 1945

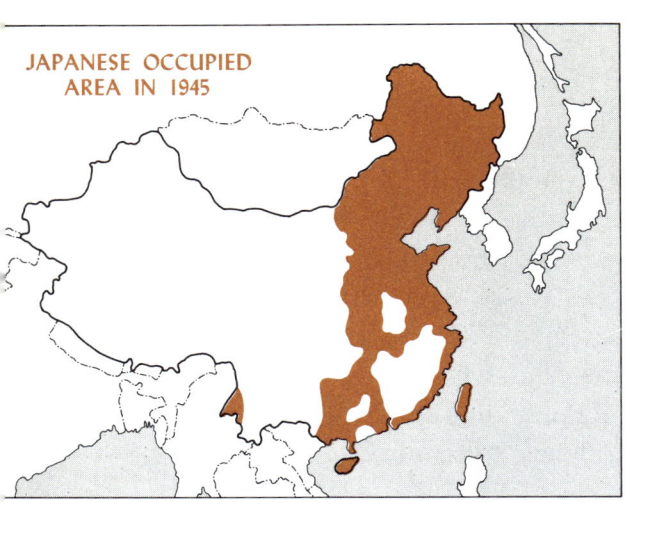

Japan invaded China in 1931 by sending its troops into Manchuria. By 1939 it had conquered most of eastern China. Chiang then moved his capital to Chungking and fought until the war ended. Japan held on in China until it had been defeated in World War II.

The Communist leader **Mao Tse-tung** \ˈmaud-ˈzə-ˈdung\ described guerrilla warfare as follows:

> "The enemy advances: we withdraw.
> The enemy settles down: we disturb him.
> The enemy tires: we fight him.
> The enemy retreats: we follow him."

Mao set the words to music and taught them to his army.

By 1941 there were really three Chinas, each ruled by a different group. The Japanese controlled Manchuria and the eastern cities. The Nationalists ruled in the southwest. And the Communists controlled the northwest.

On December 7, 1941, Japan attacked the United States. This brought the United States into World War II (which had begun in Europe in 1939) on the side of Britain and against Japan and Germany. China then declared war on Japan. During the war the United States and Britain sent military aid to China, most of it going by plane because Japan controlled the coastal cities. It took four years to defeat Japan. In 1945, when Japan surrendered, Japanese troops finally pulled out of China.

With the Japanese gone, two Chinas remained—the Nationalist and the Communist. Now the question was, Which group of Chinese would control the government?

THE COMMUNIST TRIUMPH

As it turned out, victory in China's civil war finally went to the Communists. Historians are still arguing about the reasons why.

Nationalist Weaknesses

One reason for the Nationalist defeat was the war with Japan. After the Japanese took over Manchuria, they controlled about 40 per cent of China's coal and iron ore and 70 per cent of its electric power. This was a severe blow to China's growing industries. Even more damaging was Japan's conquest of China's eastern cities. The Nationalists lost almost all the territory that they had gained in China since 1928.

In addition, as the war went on, many Nationalist leaders forgot about Confucius's teaching that government officials should be honest. Instead of dividing whatever food was available, they sold it at high prices. Poor people could not afford these prices. Thousands starved to death, while government officials became rich.

The Nationalist Army was no more honest than the government. Instead of paying the soldiers, many army officers kept the payroll money for themselves. Instead of using medical supplies to help the wounded, the officers stole the supplies and sold them. They put money ahead of loyalty to their troops and party.

Furthermore, the Nationalist Army was exhausted after years of warfare. It had lost 3,000,000 men in combat against the Japanese. Many Kuomintang soldiers did not want to fight any longer, especially not against their own people. Tens of thousands of Kuomintang soldiers deserted. Some went over to the Communists. Others went home.

Communist Strengths

One of the main reasons for the victory of the Communists was the way they behaved in contrast to the Nationalists. Red Army soldiers paid farmers for food instead of taking it. Officers of the Red Army wore the same kind of clothes and lived in the same way as the ordinary soldiers. Mao Tse-tung cultivated his own field of cabbages. The Communist leaders were honest.

The Communists were well liked by the Chinese peasants. Usually, when the Red Army conquered an area, it found that about half the peasants rented rather than owned their farms. The Communists began a system of **land reform.** They told the farmers that the landowner was to blame for the fact that they were so poor.

"If you owned the land yourself," they said, "and did not have to pay rent, you would be much better off. The Communist party will take the land away from the landowner and give it to you." Then the Communists would burn the landowner's title deed. Land reform won many peasants to the Communist side.

Mao Tse-tung, Communist Leader

The Communists practiced land reform because of the teachings of their leader Mao Tse-tung. Mao was born in South China in 1893, the son of a farmer. Mao combined working in the fields and going to school until he was sixteen. Then he left home. He continued his studies and also took many walking trips over different provinces of China. He learned a great deal about the life of the farmers on these trips. Later he went to Peking, where he got a job as an assistant librarian at the National University.

While in Peking, Mao read a book called *The Communist Manifesto*. He accepted its ideas and became a Communist.

That same year, 1921, he helped found the Chinese Communist party at a meeting in Shanghai. After Chiang Kai-shek turned the Communists out of the Kuomintang in 1927, Mao became the Communist party's leader.

Instead of giving the most help to city people, as the Nationalists did, Mao decided to begin with the peasants. The most important place for reforms, Mao thought, was in the villages, where 90 per cent of the people lived. He knew the problems of the farmers from his studies and his travels. He also knew China's history. And he probably remembered that two great dynasties, the Han and the Ming, came to power because of peasant revolts.

Mao believed that the Communists could defeat the Nationalists if they won the support of China's farmers. He convinced the other Communist leaders that he was right. From 1927 on, the Communist party found ways to help the farmers. The most important way was by giving them land. The Communists also set up schools to teach the farmers how to read and write.

The Final Struggle

In 1927 the Communists fled to a hilly area in South China. Chiang dispatched one army after another against them. He finally succeeded in cornering them in 1934. Led by Mao Tse-tung, the Communists escaped and set out on the Long March to North China. There Mao and his followers fought against the Japanese and waited for another chance to take over China's government.

Japan's defeat in 1945 was the signal for the start of a race between the Communists and the Nationalists to control China. Fighting between the two groups broke out almost immediately. The United States sent officials to try to persuade the two groups to work together. They agreed to try, but it soon became clear that they were too far apart in their ideas ever to agree.

For four years Nationalist and Communist armies struggled for control. The Nationalists numbered about 3,000,000 men, armed with weapons from the United States. The Communists numbered about 1,000,000 men, armed mostly with weapons which the Japanese had left behind when they fled from Manchuria.

Gradually the Communists assumed the lead in the struggle. Near the end of 1948 a battle raged for more than two months in the southeastern part of the Yellow Plain. When the battle was over, much of the Nationalist power had been destroyed. The Communists marched south, taking over the country as they went. In April, 1949, they captured Nanking, the Nationalist capital. Other important cities also fell to the Communists.

Chiang Kai-shek and the Nationalists now realized that they were defeated. They escaped to the island of Formosa, an island 100 miles off the southeast coast. There they set up a national government with Chiang as president.

In Peking on October 1, 1949, Mao Tse-tung proclaimed the birth of the People's Republic of China. This is the official name of Communist China. Standing on a balcony where emperors had stood before, Mao addressed a cheering throng.

"The New China is here," he said. "Let us clap our hands and welcome it. Raise both your hands. The New China is ours."

Old China was gone. Neither Sun Yat-sen, Yuan Shih-k'ai, the warlords, nor the Nationalists had been able to build a successful new China. Now the Communists had their chance to build a strong and modern nation on the Chinese mainland.

Unit 4

I. Word Study

Match each word in **Column 1** with its meaning in **Column 2**.

Column 1	Column 2
1. tribute	a. National People's Party
2. land reform	b. A habit-forming drug
3. opium	c. Headquarters of a foreign nation
4. Kuomintang	d. A tax on goods
5. peace treaty	e. Generals who held power by force
6. tariff	f. Agreement between nations to end war
7. guerrilla war	g. A tax paid to another nation
8. legation	h. A system of land redistribution
9. treaty port	i. Undercover fighting by small bands
10. warlords	j. A coastal city where trade is carried on by agreement between nations

II. Questions for Discussion

1. Why Europeans wanted more Chinese trade in the late 1700's and 1800's.
2. Why the Manchus could not meet Europe's challenge.
3. Why Sun Yat-sen is called the "Father of the Revolution."
4. How Sun was able to get help from the Soviet Union.
5. How Mao Tse-tung became the Communist leader.
6. Why the Communists finally won the war.

III. Things to Do

1. In 1839 a Chinese official destroyed chests of opium brought by British ships to Canton. In an American history look up the Boston Tea Party. Compare the two events. Did both lead to war?

2. Pretend you were a newspaper correspondent in China in 1945-1949. Write a series of telegrams reporting events as they happened.

U.P.I. Photo

These Chinese soldiers are marching in a mass rally and demonstration in Shensi Province in central China. Half a million Chinese attended the rally.

UNIT 5 *Under the Red Star*

When the Communists took over mainland China in 1949, they began another Long March. This time their goal was to build a strong, modern nation. They have worked hard against great difficulties, trying to put into practice new and untried ideas. Only during the years between 1950 and 1960, when the Soviet Union sent them machines and engineers, have they had any outside help.

How are the Communists succeeding? Let us take a close look at life in China today.

LIFE IN CHINA'S COUNTRYSIDE

As you read earlier, about 90 per cent of Chinese people—or about 675,000,000 persons—live in villages. The villagers are mostly farmers. There are about 600,000 villages on the Chinese mainland.

Changes on the Land

One of the main reasons why the Communists defeated the Nationalists was their program of land reform. When the Communists conquered an area of China, they either lowered rents or took land from the landlords and divided it among the men who were farming it. Then, in 1950, the Communist government issued a land distribution law for the entire country. Millions of peasants became landowners for the first time in their lives.

Unfortunately, China has less than half an acre of cropland for each peasant. As a result, after the land was given out, the farms were so small that they could barely feed a family. They could not produce a surplus.

The Communist government wanted farmers to produce as large a surplus as possible. First, it wanted to make certain that every Chinese had enough to eat. In addition to feeding themselves, the farmers had to produce food for the people in cities. Also, the government wanted to buy machines from other countries to aid farm production. The countries selling the machines would take such products as tea and silk in exchange. So the farmers who raised silkworms and had tea plantations were expected to increase their production.

What was to be done? The first thing the Communists did to produce more was to form **cooperatives** \kō-ˈäp-ə-rət-ivz\. In a cooperative the small farms were put together and cultivated like a single large farm. The farmers shared whatever tools and animals they owned. At the end of the season they divided the harvest. The amount of produce each farmer received for his own use depended on the amount of land, tools, and animals he had contributed.

The cooperatives helped China's farmers to grow more crops. But the production was still too low. So the government set up **collectives** \kə-ˈlek-tivz\ in place of cooperatives. On a collective, farmers no longer owned their land, except for a very small plot. Instead, the land belonged to the collective. So did the tools, animals, seeds, and fertilizer. The collective was run by managers who had the same kind of responsibility as factory managers in a factory. They decided what crops to plant and in which fields to plant them. After the harvest, the managers saw to it that the crop was sold and that the farmers were paid for their work. The amount of money and produce each farmer received depended on how much work he had done.

The collectives helped China's farmers grow larger crops. This was mostly a result of building more irrigation projects. In the past it had been difficult to increase irrigation. Some land was so far away from a proposed new canal that the farmer owning the land would not benefit from it. So he saw no reason to spend time digging an irrigation canal. Often the only way to get such a canal constructed was by drafting labor.

Under the Communist system of collectives, however, certain people were appointed full-time construction workers. They dug ditches, built dams and reservoirs, and in other ways improved the irrigation system. The collective paid them for their work just as it paid the farmers.

These men and women are working on a conservation project on a commune near the Yellow Sea. Under expert advice barren land became productive.

Eastfoto

In 1958 the government decided to go one step further. It organized **communes** \ˈkäm-ˌyünz\. A commune was like a very large collective. But it was something more. On a commune, the people not only worked together in the fields, but families also shared many living arrangements with other families.

For example, a commune had a central dining hall where every member ate his meals. People could no longer eat at home. Young children were put in a nursery so that their mothers could be sent to work in the fields. Home life was disorganized.

The pay that a worker received was no longer based on how much work he did. Everyone, regardless of whether he was a hard worker or a lazy worker, received the same amount of food, clothing, medical care, and money.

Did the communes succeed? Not at all.

The good farmers resented the fact that the poor farmers received the same rewards as they did. Women were unhappy because they spent less time with their children. Meals in the commune dining halls were often poorly cooked. But the cooks could not be fired, so there was no way to make them improve.

In addition, the managers of the communes had been chosen because they were good Communists not because they were good farm managers. Many of them made poor decisions about what crops to plant and where to plant them. Some managers were so eager to make a good showing with party leaders that they overworked farmers to the point of collapse.

Crop production under the commune system did not increase. What *did* increase was unhappiness among the people. In fact, there was so much resentment and grumbling that the government gave up the plan. Only three years after they were set up, the communes were, for all practical purposes, abolished. The government kept the name "commune," but it went back to the system of collectives. It even divided some of the large collectives. The farming was still run by a manager, but the land was owned by the 20 to 40 families who farmed it. The schools, stores, workshops, and medical clinics were still run by the commune management.

Today farmers in China have small plots of their own. They plant and tend their plots after they finish their regular work in the fields. In their gardens some farmers grow vegetables for their own use. Others sell their produce in nearby cities. Families now may eat at home. Children no longer have to be placed in nurseries. And women are not required to work in the fields.

Since 1961 crop production in China has gone up. Vegetables and grain are usually plentiful, and many Chinese eat chicken or pork four or five times a month. It would be hard to find a fat Chinese, but it would also be hard to find a hungry one. This is a tremendous accomplishment for a nation where millions of people used to starve to death in years of severe flood or drought.

On the other hand, many farmers are not satisfied. They would rather have their own small farms than work as commune employees. They show this by the extra care they give to their little gardens. The crops they raise on these home plots are much larger in proportion than those produced on the large fields of the commune.

The Red October Commune

Mr. and Mrs. Tung Teh and their four children live in the Red October Commune in North China. About 2,500 families, or about 13,000 persons, live in the commune. Half of them are under 15 years of age.

Eight of the nine villages in the Red October Commune have changed little since Mr. and Mrs. Tung were children. The villagers still live in three-generation houses made of sundried brick. The women still cook noodles and vegetables in iron pots over mud stoves. Families still sleep huddled on k'angs that are heated by a slow fire underneath. Walls of packed earth still line the unpaved streets. After nightfall the villages are still unlighted.

Only in the main village of the commune have things changed. But the changes in the main village are many. Here is the commune's assembly hall where political meetings and shows are held. Here is the commune's store, which sells goods ranging from sewing machines and shovels to good-luck charms for babies and plaster heads of Mao Tse-tung. Here is the commune's medical clinic. Here also is a workshop that turns out hoes and plows for the commune's farmers. In this village, too, is the showpiece of the Red October Commune—a high school. The people are proud of the school's library and its exhibit of stuffed birds and animals which they made themselves.

Mr. Tung, like most adults in the Red October Commune, is a farmer. He spends most of his time in the fields—planting, weeding, cleaning mud from the irrigation ditches, or feeding the mules. The mules are used to plow and haul on the commune. Mr. Tung usually works from daybreak to dusk, with one day off each week.

Two evenings a week Mr. and Mrs. Tung attend political meetings in the commune's assembly hall. The meetings are really pep rallies. A football coach in the United States encourages his team to go out on the field and win the game. A commune chairman in China encourages farmers to work harder in order to produce more than the year before. The chairman and assistants are chosen by commune members.

Sometimes the political meetings include a movie or a play put on by a group of touring actors. Mr. Tung's favorite play is called *Two Sisters in a Mountain Village*. In this play the older sister is the heroine. She likes the commune and spends her free time planting fruit trees on the mountainside. The younger sister spends her free time admiring herself in a mirror and wishing she could live in the city. The play aims to show that she has not yet learned the right way to behave. Mr. Tung likes the play because it shows how good it is to live in a commune.

Mrs. Tung, who is a hygiene teacher, has a somewhat different point of view. Several years ago she took a three-month course in Peking on disease prevention and first aid. She enjoyed life in the city—its comforts, its excitement, and the new people she met. But she realizes how valuable her job is to the people who live in the Red October Commune.

To her classes, made up of adults, Mrs. Tung explains what bacteria are and how they cause disease. She shows posters about how important it is to wash fruits and vegetables before eating them. The young people learn such things in school. But most of the older people have never been to school.

Mr. and Mrs. Tung have four children. Their older son, who is 17, is a farmer like his father. Their younger son, who is 16, works in the commune's workshop. Their two daughters, aged 12 and 10, are still in school.

The Tungs are an average family who live in an average commune. They live with Mrs. Tung's mother in a three-room house. They own a sewing machine, two thermos bottles, and a clock. They are saving money to buy a radio next year. In four years time, if all goes well, they will be able to buy a bicycle.

Tilling the Good Earth

Communes are new in China. But certain things about life on the farm have scarcely changed from the days of Confucius. Two things in particular are as true today as they were 2,000 years ago. The first is that nothing is wasted. The second is that most of the work is done by human labor.

Chinese farmers use every bit of land available. Land beside the road is never unused because farmers plow right up to the road's edge. They plant crops on the narrow dikes between the flooded rice fields, and they farm the hillside terraces all the way to the top. In some places the hills are so steep that farmers cannot stand erect in the fields. They plant and weed and harvest crops by working on their hands and knees.

Chinese farmers never discard "night soil," or human wastes. They use it on their fields for fertilizer. There are few modern sewers in China at the present time. Instead, special workmen go from house to house collecting the daily wastes. They take the wastes out to the fields and dump them in large manure pits. Later the manure is removed from the pits and spread over the land before it is plowed.

The Chinese use other sources of fertilizer, too. They scrape mud from the bottom of canals and ponds because it is rich in animal and fish droppings. School children compete to see who can collect the most horse and buffalo dung. The teacher loudly praises the pupil with the largest sack.

Chinese farmers would be horrified at our practice of burning leaves which drop from trees in the fall. The Chinese carefully collect the fallen leaves. They also collect dried stalks and twigs that break off from trees and bushes. They place all this matter in a pile to decay. The next year they use it to restore plant food to the soil.

Paris Match from Pictorial Parade

Heavy loads like this must be pulled by people in China because the nation lacks machines and draft animals to do the work. Notice the number of barrels piled on the carts. Does this tell you that the load is heavy?

The main source of power on China's farms is human muscles. Chinese farmers themselves still do most of the work of pushing, pulling, and carrying. Just as in Old China, people today pull carts, pedal waterwheels, and stoop over, hour after hour, setting out rice plants in the mud.

Some farm machinery is now used on the communes. Most of the machines are tractors in the wheat fields of North China and pumps in the rice fields of South China. There are not enough machines to replace hand labor because China at present produces only a limited number of machines. To get more machines, the government must import them from other nations. But machines are expensive, and China is still a poor country. It does not have many surplus products to sell, so it can buy only a few machines at a time.

Even more important, if large numbers of farmers were replaced by machines, it would "break people's rice bowls." Suppose, for example, that the managers of the Red October Commune bought a tractor-driven plow. Such a plow would do the work of 20 farmers. One of the farmers could become

99

The commune workers shown here are sorting rice seed to be used in planting next year. The largest whole grains of rice are selected because they make the best seed.

U.P.I. Photo

the tractor driver and continue to work. But the other 19 farmers would be unemployed. Not only that. They would not be able to find other work because China, as yet, has very few job openings in either industry or services.

LIFE IN CHINA'S CITIES

China has many cities. Twenty of them are giants, each with more than 1,000,000 inhabitants. Most of the cities are medium-sized, with populations that range from 50,000 to 500,000. Shanghai, Peking, and Chungking are the largest.

Let us take a look at the capital, Peking. Peking, like most Chinese cities, is a mixture of the old and the new. It has its old sections which recall the past. It has new sections which are very modern.

A View of Peking

Peking's old streets, called **hutungs** \hù-'dunz\, are narrow, curving alleyways, unpaved and unlighted. Its new streets are broad, paved avenues that run straight south and north or east and west. They are lined with lamp posts and, here and there, with newly planted willow and maple trees.

100

Peking's old buildings turn gray and windowless walls to the street. The windows of these buildings are covered with oiled paper rather than glass, and they open onto an inner courtyard. If the building is a private house, the courtyard contains the family's stove. Old buildings are only one story high. Since Peking stands on flat land, a two-story building would have enabled tenants to look down on the emperor's palace. And no one was allowed to look down on the ruler of the Chinese empire!

Peking's new buildings are usually four stories high. Most are built of red brick or yellow stucco, with glass windows facing the street. Apartment houses often have a balcony for each apartment as well as running water and an indoor stove.

Peking begins to wake up at five o'clock in the morning. First come the street cleaners sweeping the avenues. Most of the cleaners are women. They work in a line that stretches from one side of a street to the other. Swish, swish—the brooms move together in a kind of rhythm.

Sellers of noodles and vegetables are crying their wares in sing-song voices. Dumplings sizzle over charcoal fires, ready to be sold to hungry passersby. Fishmongers set up their water tubs and get ready for their customers.

By six o'clock factory and office workers are on their way to their jobs. Most people walk or ride bicycles. Few Chinese own cars, and there are not many trucks, buses, and official cars in Peking. In fact, automobiles are so scarce that they have the right of way. Whenever a car comes down the street, the policeman immediately changes the traffic signal to green so the car can go through.

As the morning wears on, Peking's streets fill with **pedicabs** and carts. A pedicab is a tricycle with a platform built over the two back wheels. The driver pedals it just like a

U.P.I. Photo

This is the main railway station in Peking. Many people come and go there daily because the capital is a busy city. Mao Tse-tung's picture reminds them that China is Communist. Pictures of Mao are seen everywhere.

bicycle. A cart is pulled by three or more workers, tugging on ropes. All sorts of goods—even bulky electrical machines or heavy sacks of rice—are moved by pedicabs and carts. In transportation, just as in farming, China uses manpower much more than machine power.

In the late afternoon parents and children stroll together along the avenues. Grandparents wheel their grandchildren in bamboo baby carriages. Here is a troop of soldiers stepping smartly along. There is a line of youngsters with their teacher on their way to visit a museum.

When night falls, the old sections of Peking turn dark, except for flickering charcoal fires. If the weather is pleasant, people sit in the alleyways, smoking pipes and watching the moon over the tiled roofs of the buildings.

In the new sections electric lights gleam from apartment windows, lamp posts, store fronts, and advertising signs. Workers shop in the department stores, which stay open every night, or practice military drills in the city's great square.

By midnight Peking is once again asleep. All traffic has stopped. The only sound is the occasional chirp of a cricket.

Peking Workers

Peking is one of China's leading industrial cities. Let us listen to a Peking worker as he tells his story.

"My name is **Hsu Chang-do** \\'shü-'jäng-'dō\\. I am 28 years old, and I work at Peking Machine Tool Plant Number One, where I operate a lathe. My wife, **Kwei-ying** \\'gwā-'ying\\, also works at this factory. She greases machines before they are packed for shipment.

"Both Kwei-ying and I work the early morning shift from 6:00 A.M. to 2:30 P.M. We have half an hour for lunch, which we eat in the factory canteen. After work I attend school for two hours. I am studying Mandarin, arithmetic, and 'general culture.' I grew up during the civil war and had only two years of regular school before I began working. Now I am in the sixth grade and can read more than 1,500 characters.

"While I am in class, Kwei-ying takes our two children home from the factory nursery, buys our groceries, and cleans our two-room apartment. We live in a housing project recently built by the factory where we work. One of our rooms is used as a living room, dining room, and bedroom. The other room is a kitchen with running water and gas for cooking. We also have our own inside toilet.

"Our apartment shows that my wife likes bright colors. She covered the light bulbs with yellow paper shades and hung pictures of flowers on the walls. She painted the table and four chairs orange. She even embroidered a green cotton cover for our radio set.

As all Chinese workers must, these people are attending a political meeting where they study Mao Tse-tung's writings and discuss Communist ideas.

"At least one night a week, and sometimes two, Kwei-ying and I attend political meetings at the plant. The meetings usually last an hour and a half to three hours. We sit around a table and take turns reading from the writings of Chairman Mao Tse-tung. Then we discuss the meaning of what we have read. Each of us has to give a six-minute talk on how the thoughts of Chairman Mao can help us do a better job.

"Kwei-ying and I have the same day off from work each week. We usually spend it at the factory recreation center. Her favorite sport is swimming. Mine is ping-pong. Recently I have begun playing basketball.

"Sometimes the factory organizes trips for workers and their families. We crowd into trucks and ride out to the Great Wall, singing all the way. Before we know it, the three-hour drive is over. Then we climb to the top of the wall. When we reach the top, some friends and I play cards.

"Kwei-ying does not go to the top of the wall. She usually sits with our children in one of the new teahouses. There she rests, sips tea, and gazes at the view of the wall and the mountain peaks beyond.

"I am really very fortunate. I have a good job, a new apartment, and a wife whom I chose myself. I have only one problem. Both of our children are girls. True, the Communist party says:

> First born—good,
> Second born—enough,
> Third born—too much,
> Fourth born—sinful.

But a man is not really a man unless he has a son."

A Peking Factory

Peking Machine Tool Plant Number One is a typical Chinese factory. It is owned by the government, which built it in 1952 with the help of Russian engineers. It is run by **Feng Po-ta** \\'fung-'bō-'tä\\, appointed by the government as factory manager. Mr. Feng decides what job each of the factory's workers should do. He is also in charge of the factory canteen, the factory recreation center, and the factory housing project.

Mr. Feng's most important task is increasing production. He is always putting up posters urging workers to turn out more goods. Each month he awards a medal to the best workers and displays their pictures on the factory bulletin board. A worker who develops a better method of working receives a bonus. So does a worker who turns out more than his share.

Mr. Feng also spends time trying to make improvements. Peking Machine Tool Plant Number One was one of the first factories in China to set up a work-study school.

The teen-aged students in the school are all children of factory workers. The students spend half their time in the plant and half in the classroom. Experienced workers like Mr. and Mrs. Hsu teach them how to operate machines and what to do to keep machines running properly. In the classroom they study politics and technical subjects such as engineering and mathematics. At the end of four years they will be skilled workers with an education equal to about two years of high school. And most of them will keep right on working in Peking Machine Tool Plant Number One.

USING NATURAL RESOURCES

China's industries have grown greatly since 1949. The Communists have constructed many factories. They have tried different ways of encouraging people to produce more. And they have taught millions of workers how to use modern machines. But to become an industrial power, China must make full use of its abundant natural resources.

China's Industries

Marco Polo described the Chinese as "the people who burn black stones." The Chinese were the first people in the world, so far as we know, to burn coal to produce heat.

Coal is China's most abundant natural resource. Most of its coalfields are in the northeast, in what was formerly called Manchuria. China also contains sizable deposits of iron ore and is developing a flourishing steel industry.

The leading steel producer is the northeastern city of **Anshan** \\'än-shan\\, which turns out about half the nation's steel. Most of Anshan's mills were built by the Japanese during the 1930's, when they controlled Manchuria. After Japan withdrew from China in 1945, the Chinese—with Russian help—expanded and modernized the mills. Other important steel centers are Mukden, also in the northeast, and Wuhan, on the Yangtze River.

In addition to coal and iron ore China contains good supplies of **tungsten, antimony,** and tin. Tungsten and tin are used in making steel. Antimony is used in printing.

China's farm products are used in the nation's oldest and largest industry, making cloth. The materials used in cloth making are mostly cotton and silk.

Chinese farmers grow large quantities of cotton. Its quality is low, however, because they use only their poor soil for cotton. They save the more fertile soil for food crops. Silk thread, as you read earlier, comes from the cocoon of the silk-moth caterpillar. The caterpillar eats mulberry leaves before it spins its cocoon. Mulberry bushes are common throughout the Yangtze delta, where they grow on the dikes between the flooded fields of rice.

China has more raw materials for industry than any other nation in Asia. But it lacks two kinds of power needed to develop its raw materials: electricity and oil.

CHINA: NATURAL RESOURCES

- ♦ Antimony
- 🗼 Oil
- △ Lead
- 🏠 Coal
- ➚ Tin
- ○ Waterpower
- 🏠 Iron Ore
- ▭ Tungsten
- 🌲 Forests

The Chinese produce electricity by burning coal to heat water to make steam. The steam is used to turn the generators that produce electricity. The Chinese use about 75 per cent of their yearly coal production to produce electricity. Yet the amount of electricity produced is very small compared to China's needs.

Production Problems

Why don't the Chinese use the power of falling water to produce electricity since they cannot get enough from steam power? After all, the Hwang Ho and the Yangtze Kiang, as well as smaller rivers, contain hundreds of waterfalls. The

This huge reservoir, which is part of an anti-flood project on the Huai River, was built by human labor. Since China lacks machines, it must depend on its vast reserves of man power to do much of the needed construction.

Eastfoto

answer is that building dams and power plants is expensive, and China lacks the money to construct them. The government is building as many dams and power plants as it can afford. But many years will go by before it has enough.

Another problem is that the waterfalls are hundreds of miles distant from most of the cities. Even if China were to build all the dams and power plants it needs, it would still have to bring the electricity to homes and factories. This would mean constructing a nation-wide system of power lines, another expensive undertaking.

China has sizable oil deposits. Like the waterfalls, however, they are far away from most of the cities. Before any large amounts of oil can be produced, China must first construct roads and railroads to carry workers and equipment to the oil fields. Then it will have to build towns where the workers can live. Finally, it will have to build pipelines to carry the oil from the fields and refineries to market. The government is working on all these things. But many years will go by before China has enough oil to fuel the tractors and trucks it needs.

THE GOVERNMENT OF COMMUNIST CHINA

The People's Republic of China was born on October 1, 1949. Each year on that date the Communists have held a great parade in the main square of Peking. For two hours half a million Chinese march past their leaders. They chant "Long live Chairman Mao Tse-tung!" The marchers represent all groups—farmers, factory workers, and soldiers. Mothers wheel baby carriages. Students wave banners declaring their devotion to Chairman Mao. Gymnasts and dancers perform. And high overhead, thousands of red balloons soar upward.

What kind of government have the Communists set up in China? And what is the role of the Red Army, which brought the Communist government into power?

How the Communist Party Works

China's constitution, which was written in 1954, provides for a Chairman, or President, to head the nation. It also provides for a National People's Congress and a State Council. The Congress is supposed to make the nation's laws. The Council is supposed to carry out the laws.

Studying the constitution, however, tells very little about what China's government is really like. The reason is that the members of the National People's Congress and the State Council have no real power. They do only what the Communist party wants them to do.

Only a small percentage of the Chinese—approximately 17,500,000 persons—are members of the Communist party. It is not easy to become a member. First, a person has to be sponsored by two party members. Then he has to go through a one-year testing period, at the end of which he must pass an examination on the principles of communism. Lastly, he has to swear to obey the party's orders. A party member may argue with other party members before a decision is made but never afterwards. After the candidate is finally accepted, he swears his loyalty to the party and receives a membership card that he always carries with him.

Chinese who join the Communist party are expected to set a good example for all the people. They are expected to be honest and hardworking and to consider the nation's and the party's welfare more important than their own.

The Communist party is not the only political party in China. There are eight other parties with a membership of several hundred thousand, but they have no real power.

The Communist party chooses the candidates in all elections. The candidates are either party members or else very loyal to the party and what it stands for. The Communist party draws up the nation's laws. The only thing the National People's Congress does is to vote "Yes" for the laws drawn up by the party.

In one way the Communist government is like the government of Old China. Under both governments only educated persons could be officials. In Old China, being educated meant knowing the teachings of Confucius. In Communist China, being educated means knowing the teachings of Karl Marx and Mao Tse-tung.

What Communists Believe

The ideas upon which communism is based developed in the mind of a young German named Karl Marx. Karl's father, a successful lawyer, sent him to the university to study law. But the young man found himself more interested in history and philosophy. His mind dwelled upon the wrongs the poor had always suffered and upon the plight of workingmen in his own time.

In those days there were no labor laws. People were expected to work 12 and 14 hours a day and to accept whatever wages factory owners were willing to pay. Even small children were forced to work in factories.

"Why are workers the poorest class of people," Karl asked himself, "when wealth is the product of their labor? The factory owners get most of the wealth and give the workers scarcely enough to live on. The workers should not submit to this. They should unite and demand their rights."

Karl Marx became a newspaper editor. In the paper he expressed some of his ideas about the poor and the need for change. Other people were thinking along the same lines.

In 1847 a group of workingmen from different countries met in London to discuss their problems. They called themselves the Communist League. They decided that Karl Marx was the person to help them spread their ideas. So they asked him to prepare a program for their group.

Marx persuaded his friend Friedrich Engels to help him. In 1848 they published *The Communist Manifesto*. This book, with its rallying cry "Workingmen of all countries unite," marked the beginning of the Communist movement. You recall that Mao Tse-tung became a Communist after reading it. Marx and Engels later wrote several more books on communism.

What did Marx and Engels recommend? First, they said that the government should own and run all farming and industry. Everyone should work for the government, and profits should be used for the good of all the people. No one should be either rich or poor. Everyone should share and share alike.

Second, Marx and Engels said that since factory owners and landlords would not give up their property willingly, workers should revolt and take the property by force. It was the duty of the Communist party, whose members were better educated than the workers, to lead the workers in this revolution.

Third, Marx and Engels said that after a time there would no longer be any need for government at all. People would do the work they were best able to do. They would have all the things they needed for a pleasant life. And everyone would live together in peace and harmony.

How Communism Works

The Communist Manifesto helped bring about several communist revolutions. The biggest and most important were those in Russia and China. The Russian Revolution took place in 1917, more than 50 years ago. By studying the Soviet Union, we can get some idea of whether communism does what Marx and Engels hoped it would do.

In one way communism has been a success in the Soviet Union. It has become a strong and modern nation, just as China hopes to be. But in many ways the ideas of Marx and Engels turned out to be wrong. For example, there are still rich people and poor people in the Soviet Union. The difference is that today the rich people are not factory owners and landlords. They are Communist party leaders and highly skilled scientists and engineers. And instead of the power of government growing less, it has become a dictatorship. It does not permit the people to have such rights as freedom of speech and freedom of the press. We should remember, however, that neither the Russians nor the Chinese ever had these rights in the past.

The Duties of the Army

In China, from the beginning of Mao's government, the Red Army and the Communist party have worked closely together. In fact, the party created the army. During the early years Mao Tse-tung worked so closely with the Red Army commander that the Nationalists thought for awhile they were one person. During the Long March the soldiers of the Red Army were not only fighters but also political workers. They carried out the Communist program of land reform by taking land away from landlords and giving it to the peasants. After learning how to read and write themselves, they taught these skills to the farmers.

Today the Red Army is known as the People's Liberation Army. Since 1954 its members have been drafted rather than being made up of volunteers. But even today, many years after the take over, the army is still a very important part of the government.

Like all armies, the Chinese soldiers practice using different kinds of weapons and exercise to develop strong bodies. But they also work beside farmers in the fields, planting and harvesting crops. They repair roads and build dams. They help with garbage collections and food deliveries.

At times the army has still other duties. Communist party members are not supposed to argue after a decision has been reached on a question. Until the decision *is* reached, however, party members often disagree. They disagree not about communism itself but rather about whether a particular act is wise or not. In 1966 Chinese Communist party members disagreed so violently that actual fighting broke out. Production stopped in many factories as groups of workers struggled with one another for control. Mines shut down and railroads stopped running. There was even fear that crops would be left unharvested in the fields.

The army moved in and took charge. Soldiers carried out many government duties in factories, schools, and communes. They gradually succeeded in restoring order throughout the country.

The army was important in bringing the Communist government to power in 1949. In the future, it may be called upon to help one group of the Communist party win its arguments against another group.

EDUCATING PEOPLE IN COMMUNISM

The Chinese rulers know that building a strong and modern nation means more than increasing production. It also means winning the hearts and minds of the people. The Communists use many means to teach these three ideas: love of China, love of hard work, and obedience to the Communist party. School is one very important means of teaching communism.

"School Days, School Days"

The day for **Liu Sho-fang** \lĭ-ˈü-ˈshō-ˈfäng\ began like any other school day. At 6:30 A.M. the school bell, sounding through the loudspeaker, echoed up and down the narrow street. Fourteen-year-old Sho-fang tumbled out of bed, put on her blue cotton shirt and pants, and hurried off to school.

By 7:00 A.M. Sho-fang and her group were lined up in the school yard. They always began the school day by doing physical exercises. One rule of the Communists is that every Chinese must develop his muscles so that he will be able to protect his country. This includes girls also.

At 7:30 A.M. Sho-fang ate breakfast with the others in the big dining room. Then she went quickly to her classroom and joined her 50 classmates. Classes started at eight.

Sho-fang studied Mandarin, arithmetic, science, history, geography, communism, and agriculture. At noon there was an hour recess for lunch. Afternoon classes lasted until 4:00 P.M.

Wednesday afternoon was different. Then the school closed at one o'clock, and everyone who was a member attended the weekly meeting of the Communist Young Pioneers.

Sho-fang had been a member of this youth organization since she was 10. She was not accepted the first time she had tried to become a Young Pioneer. Her teacher's report had said that she sometimes fidgeted in class and looked out of the window. How quietly she had sat during class after that and what close attention she had paid! If she did not become a Young Pioneer, she knew she would not be assigned to a good high school. Then she could not go to college and study to be a doctor. She had her heart set on that.

Sho-fang had been rewarded. Now she wore the red cotton scarf that showed she was a Young Pioneer.

After school Sho-fang and her classmates usually did some kind of heavy outside work. "Every Chinese must be able to lift a shovel as well as a pen," the Communists said. One week Sho-fang might sort stacks of paper so that it could be used again. Another week she might be assigned to carry rocks to build a road. Last summer she had worked at a nearby commune, where she helped with the wheat harvest.

Today Sho-fang's teacher announced that a Communist party member had come from Peking to talk to the class. So when the four o'clock bell rang, Sho-fang and her classmates remained in their seats.

The party member was a pleasant-looking man of about 25. As he began to speak, Sho-fang had a hard time paying attention. The first half hour of a party member's speech, she thought, was always the same. The young man told them how hard Mao Tse-tung and his comrades had worked to build up the Communist party and China.

Sho-fang knew it was all true, of course, but she already knew it by heart. So, instead of listening, she daydreamed about being a doctor. She could see herself, hypodermic needle in hand, vaccinating children against smallpox or studying a blood sample under a microscope. Perhaps she might even discover a cure for some disease.

Suddenly Sho-fang sat upright in her seat. The speaker was explaining why he had come. What had he just said?

"Our comrades in Sinkiang must learn how to read and write if they are truly to take part in our glorious Communist revolution. The party has decided that everyone in this class is to become an elementary-school teacher."

"An elementary-school teacher? In faraway Sinkiang? But I want to be a doctor," Sho-fang thought, clenching her fists to stop the trembling of her hands. "I can be a good doctor. I've always done well in science. My marks are the second highest in class. Also, I'm local secretary of the Young Pioneers."

"We will do whatever is necessary for the good of our country!" she heard the teacher say. A few pupils repeated the words. Then more voices joined in until the room was ringing with the noise.

Sho-fang swallowed. Then, slowly, she joined in the chorus. "We will do whatever is necessary for the good of our country!"

Molding Minds

Chinese children begin to learn about communism in nursery school, which they may enter at the age of three. Nursery-school children do not have toys or crayons of their own. Toys and crayons are furnished by the school. The school rules are, "Everything is *ours,* nothing is *mine.*"

At recess, they sing songs like this:

> We clap our hands we are so happy!
> The communes are so powerful!
> My father works in a factory!
> Our country is led by the Communist party!
> My brother drives the tractor,
> My sister works the loom,
> The electric light lights every household.

As children grow older, their teachers explain Communist ideas to them. They tell stories about heroes of the Long March and read from the writings of Mao Tse-tung. Sometimes what the pupils learn is part of another subject, like

London Daily Express (from Pictorial)

In Communist China, where newsprint is scarce, walls are used as posters, and newspapers are displayed on streets for public reading. How many Chinese characters must a person know to read a newspaper?

history. Everything that happened B.L.—that is, "Before Liberation," or the Communist take-over—is described as bad (except for the peasant revolts). Everything A.L., or "After Liberation," is described as good.

Communist education does not stop with graduation from school. Mr. Tung and the other farmers in the Red October Commune attend a political meeting at least once a week. So do Mr. and Mrs. Hsu and their fellow workers in Peking Machine Tool Plant Number One.

The Communist government uses other means of reaching the people. Twice a day loudspeakers on city street corners, in railroad trains and railroad stations, and even on trees carry the Communist message. The news stories in China's newspapers and magazines, all of which are owned by the government, must follow the Communist line. Movies, plays, popular songs, and operas are all produced by the government, and all teach the Communist way of life.

"Big Brother Is Watching You"

Communist China further, like all undemocratic governments, tries to make certain that no one says or does anything of which it disapproves. How does the government do this?

Several years ago an Englishman wrote a book in which he described the world as it might be in 1984. He described a country headed by a dictator known simply as Big Brother. Big Brother held his political power by using a two-way television screen. Every room in every building in the nation had such a screen. In this way Big Brother and his associates could see and hear what everybody was doing and saying. It was easy for Big Brother to spot anyone who disagreed with his ideas.

The Chinese Communist government does not have two-way television screens. But it does have millions of people like Mrs. **Chien Feng-shu** \ˈjē-äng ˈfung ˈshü\.

Mrs. Chien is the chairman of a street committee in Peking. She was elected chairman by the committee members, who in turn were elected by the residents of the street. Mrs. Chien, who is 58, is considered too old for a factory job. As a street committee chairman, she does not do heavy work.

Mrs. Chien serves partly as a street janitor. She reports uncollected garbage and leaking roofs to the proper authorities. Her real job, however, is to keep an eye on her neighbors.

Suppose Mrs. Chien visits another apartment and sees that it has not been cleaned properly. She lectures the housewife on her sloppiness. If a teacher or office worker has not volunteered to do heavy labor during the weekend, she upbraids him publicly in a loud voice. If she overhears someone complaining about the government, she reports him to party authorities. She is always reminding youngsters of

U.P.I. Photo

All farm communes have a village where the commune members shop. This shopping street is in a village that is part of a commune near Shanghai.

their duty to report to her if their parents say anything against communism.

There was a saying in Old China: "The sky is high, the emperor is far away." It meant that the national government had little to do with the day-to-day life of the people. The emperor made the laws which the chin-shih carried out. But the laws at that time dealt only with such matters as taxes and army service. All other problems were handled by family heads in the villages.

Just the opposite is true today. The Peking government is interested in everything the people do. It assigns jobs, supervises their work, requires them to attend political gatherings, and allows them to read only what the government approves. It also checks up on their conversation. It not only controls people's actions but even tries to control their thoughts. While China remains communist, no matter who the head of the party is, the communist way of life will be taught and its ideas enforced.

I. Word Study

Three of the words in each list below belong in the same group. Tell which word does not belong.
1. Tungsten, antimony, coal, iron
2. Commune, cooperative, collective, canteen
3. Avenue, k'ang, hutung, street
4. Cart, pedicab, truck, sampan
5. Young Pioneer, Communist League, Communist party, Kuomintang

II. Questions for Discussion

1. Why does China use more man power than machines?
2. What is the relationship between dams and increasing crops? Between building dams and expanding industry?
3. What does the saying "to break people's rice bowls" mean?
4. Why is Peking said to be a mixture of old and new?

III. Making Comparisons

A. Some of the statements below apply to the **Li Family** (Old China) and some to the **Tung Family** (Communist China). Make two columns on your paper, and indicate the column where each statement applies.
1. Several generations live together in the same house.
2. Children obey their parents without question.
3. Children are expected to start work at the age of six.
4. The father makes decisions for the family.
5. The teachings of Confucius are followed.
6. The government is more important than the family.
7. Marriages are arranged between families.
8. Young people are encouraged not to marry young.

B. Compare the thoughts of Mao Tse-tung with the teachings of Confucius in the influence each has had on Chinese life.

UNIT 6

Rice is the main crop on Formosa just as it is in South China, on the mainland. Both men and women work at the rice harvest, using the old methods of gathering the grain. The mountains in the distance are typical of the island scenery.

Formosa and

The first Europeans to see the island of Formosa were Portuguese sailors in the 1500's. The island's forested cliffs, sparkling waterfalls, and green plains sloping to the sea so impressed the sailors that they exclaimed "Ilha formosa!—Beautiful island!" Most Europeans have called it Formosa ever since. To the Chinese and other Asians, however, it is known as Taiwan.

Since 1949 Formosa has had several other names as well. These include Free China, Nationalist China, and the Republic of China. The reason is that Formosa is the seat of the Nationalist government.

122

Photos from Chinese Information Service

Taipei, capital of Formosa, is a city with modern buildings and industries. This park, which is in the heart of the city, has gay Chinese pavilions to provide relaxation for workers. Pottery making, an ancient Chinese art, is carried on in this Taipei factory. Notice the landscape designs on the vases.

the Nationalists

A GOVERNMENT IN EXILE

Formosa was a part of the Chinese empire from the early years of the Manchu dynasty. After a war in 1895 China yielded it to Japan. Fifty years later, at the end of World War II, the island was returned to China and became the nation's smallest province.

In 1947 the first wave of Nationalist refugees arrived from the mainland. Two years later, after the Communist takeover, came 600,000 Nationalist troops led by Chiang Kai-shek. They brought with them the money that was left in the national treasury and several thousand packing cases

123

filled with paintings and other kinds of art. They were accompanied by 1,500,000 followers, mostly relatives of the troops.

On Formosa these refugees have built a new life for themselves and for the people of Formosa. The island has one of the highest standards of living in Asia. Let us see what farms and factories there are like.

THE GOOD EARTH

Almost two thirds of Formosa is covered with mountains running north and south. To the east, the mountains drop sharply into the sea. To the west, they slope into a broad coastal plain where most of the people and most of the farms are found.

Formosan farmers are fortunate. The growing season lasts the year round. This means that two and sometimes three crops a year are produced. The northern part of the island has heavy rains in the winter, but the summers are dry. The south has heavy rains in the summer, but the winters are dry. During the dry seasons irrigation canals and ditches carry water from mountain streams down to the coastal plain. The irrigation system was developed by the Japanese and has been expanded by the Chinese Nationalists.

Formosan farmers are modern. They use chemical fertilizers as well as human wastes to improve the fertility of the soil. They are gradually replacing their water buffaloes with small power-driven machines from Japan. The machines run on natural gas, of which the island has a good supply. They do the work much faster than buffaloes do, and they plow deeper furrows in the ground. The result is that Formosa has been steadily producing more and better crops on the same amount of land.

Chinese Information Service

This photograph shows men harvesting rice in the southern part of Formosa. The rice crop is abundant here. Why do men wear this style of hat?

The leading crop in Formosa, as it is in South China, is rice. Farmers are able to grow more rice than they need. They sell their surplus to Japan and to nations in southeast Asia. Sugar cane and sweet potatoes are other leading crops. The Formosans make money by refining sugar and selling it abroad. Home-grown pineapples and mushrooms are canned in local factories. Some of the best-tasting tea in the world is grown on Formosa.

Most Formosan farmers own their farms. This was not always so. When the island was ruled by Japan, the Japanese owned most of the land. Formosan farmers had to pay more than half of their crops for rent. Many spent their whole lifetime in debt. After 1945, however, the Nationalist government—with the advice and help of the United States—began making changes. First, it lowered farm rents. Next, it took over plantations, divided them into small farms of less than three acres, and sold the farms to the people at low prices. Finally, it limited the amount of land that a single farmer could own.

Formosan farmers have much better houses than farmers on the Chinese mainland. Most of their homes are made of bright red bricks, with tiled or thatched roofs. Glass windows are common as are electricity and running water. Many of the people own bicycles or motorcycles. Well-to-do families, often called "five-thing families," are now common. The "five things" are a motorcycle, a radio, a sewing machine, a rice thresher run by a foot pedal, and an electric rice cooker.

All Formosan children attend elementary school for six years and junior high school for three years. You might find some things about a Formosan school somewhat unusual. For one thing, all pupils wear a special school uniform. For another thing, pupils usually do their studying out loud in sing-song voices. When 50 pupils all recite their lessons at the same time, they make a great deal of noise.

Formosa's public-school system, which was started by the Japanese, has been expanded by the Nationalists. About half the pupils attend senior high school, and about one-fourth go to college. Most Formosans can read and write.

These young people are students at a college near Taipei. The architecture is interesting because it has copied some features used in the ancient Chinese palaces.

Chinese Information Service

Chinese Information Service

This plant in a town not far from Taipei makes fertilizer. Formosa produces all the artificial fertilizer it needs. Is this true in Communist China?

An Industrial Boom

Kao-hsiung \\'gou-shyùng\\ is a medium-sized city in the southwest part of Formosa. For many years its fine harbor was used mostly by fishermen who sailed along the coast. Its streets were filled with oxcarts and pedicabs. People bought and sold goods in tiny shops and in markets spread out on the sidewalks. Merchants even carried "traveling stores" at the ends of big sticks.

Today the harbor of Kao-hsiung is jammed with ocean freighters. Trucks and automobiles move along the wide avenues. It has large stores and office buildings.

Formosa has become one of the most prosperous areas in Asia. One reason is that the United States gave the island $1,500,000,000 aid between 1951 and 1967. The Nationalists used the money wisely, first to improve farming and then to develop industries.

Industries have been developed on Formosa because the island has good natural resources. It has much coal. It also has hundreds of streams that flow down its mountains. Both are sources of cheap electricity to run machines in factories.

In addition to good sources of power, Formosa has a large supply of workers. In fact, its population has been increasing so rapidly that today many Formosans have trouble finding work. Farms that need only three workers may have as many as seven men in the field. Stores have two or three times as many salesmen as are really needed. As a result, the people are willing to work in factories for low wages. Foreign companies are building plants on the island to make use of the cheap labor supply.

Holidays and Heroes

One of the nice things about living in Formosa is that the people enjoy two sets of holidays. They enjoy the holidays that are celebrated on the mainland and also the special holidays that honor famous people in Formosa's past.

The most important Chinese holiday is Chinese New Year's Day. Then people wear new clothes and tie gay strips of red paper on the gates of their houses. On New Year's Eve family members sit down to a big feast at midnight. Little

People of the Republic of China still find time to celebrate the old festivals. Here they are parading with a many-colored dragon made of paper. The dragon was used as a symbol of good fortune by the ancient Chinese.

Chinese Information Service

children fall asleep soon after the feast begins, but older children and grown-ups stay awake until dawn. They eat meat dumplings, white rice, tiny cakes, and toffee apples. During the next three days factories, shops, and schools are closed. People call on their relatives and friends, and children exchange wooden toys, pennies, and other gifts.

Another holiday that has been celebrated for several thousand years in China is the Dragon Boat Festival. The story is told that the Chinese poet **Ch'u Yüan** \'chü-'yü-'än\ tried to tell his king how to be a better ruler. When the king ignored his advice, Ch'u Yuan resigned his office and wrote a poem, one of the loveliest poems in the Chinese language. Then he drowned himself in a river. This happened on the fifth day of the fifth month. Ever since, on that day, groups of Chinese go out on the water in Dragon Boats to look for the poet's soul. There is an exciting Dragon Boat race.

As you might expect, a Dragon Boat is shaped to resemble a dragon. It looks like a large canoe and has a carved dragon at its front end. It holds about 20 persons. The Dragon Boat race is usually held at night, with flaming torches to light the water. People bang away at gongs and drums and set off long strings of firecrackers. They eat small cakes of rice wrapped in bamboo leaves.

Still another important Chinese holiday is "Double Ten," which comes on October 10—the tenth day of the tenth month. The Double-Ten Festival celebrates the start of the revolution that overthrew the Manchu dynasty in 1912. This holiday is very much like our Fourth of July, and the Formosans celebrate it much as we do. There are parades and speeches and firecrackers and waving flags.

The most important island holiday honors General **Koxinga** \kuk-'sing-gä\, the greatest of Formosa's heroes. Koxinga was born in 1624. His father was a famous pirate who operated off the southeast coast of China. Koxinga inherited money and also a fleet of 3,000 junks. During his youth the Manchus invaded China. Koxinga, who was loyal to the Ming emperor, fought several battles against the Manchu troops. The Manchus won, however, and in 1661 Koxinga fled with his army to Formosa.

At that time Formosa was held by the Dutch. Koxinga found two Dutch forts and several Dutch settlements there. After nearly a year's fighting, he took possession of the island and founded a kingdom. He died a year later. His grandson ruled Formosa until 1683. Then he surrendered to the Manchus. During the reign of Koxinga and his grandson, tens of thousands of Chinese came to Formosa. They brought with them their farming skills, their family system, and their respect for the teachings of Confucius.

The Formosans tell many stories about General Koxinga. According to one story, when he first landed on the island, he crossed a large beach. His footprints changed to fish and since then fishing has been one of the islanders' main occupations. According to another story, Koxinga and his army were once lost on a mountain top without any water. Koxinga thrust his sword into the ground and a river gushed out. After this the mountain was called Iron Sword Mountain.

THE NATIONALIST GOVERNMENT TODAY

Since 1949 the headquarters of the Nationalists have been in **Tai-pei** \\'tī-'pā\\, the largest city on Formosa. There is only one party which has any power—the Kuomintang—just as there is really only one party—the Communist Party—on the mainland. Unlike the Communist government, the Nationalist government does not own the newspapers, magazines, and radio stations. Even so, it does not allow any criticism of the Kuomintang or its policies.

The motto of the Nationalist government is: "Back to the mainland!" As a result, much of Formosa is a military base. The Nationalist army of 600,000 men is the fifth largest army in the world.

About 100 miles of water separate Formosa from the Chinese mainland. More important than the water barrier, however, are the ships of the United States Seventh Fleet. Since 1950 American ships have been on patrol there, preventing the Communists from invading Formosa and the Nationalists from invading the mainland.

The Seventh Fleet will certainly continue its patrol so long as Chiang Kai-shek lives, and perhaps afterwards. Eventually some decision will have to be made about the future. One way of looking at the possibilities is to learn what four people who live on Formosa think.

A Formosan Father

Yeh Joktik \ˈye-ˈjōk-tuk\ lives in Taipei. He is a 53-year-old sales clerk in a shoe store in the city. His family is one of the oldest on Formosa. His ancestors arrived with General Koxinga.

Mr. Yeh grew up while the island was ruled by the Japanese. He spoke and studied the Japanese language in school and bowed low before pictures of the Japanese emperor. Like many Formosans, he did not like the Japanese. True, they built schools, roads, and railroads, and developed an excellent irrigation system. But they owned most of the farm land and kept all the good jobs in government and industry for themselves. Japanese policemen were stationed everywhere—even in tiny villages—to watch the people.

Mr. Yeh was very happy when Formosa was returned to China in 1945. He and his three brothers went to the harbor of **Kirun** \\'ke-'rùn\\ to greet the first Nationalist officials who came ashore.

Unfortunately some greedy officials took over not only former Japanese property but Formosan property, too. They took rice away from the farmers and shipped it to the mainland where it brought a good price. The situation was so bad that within two years the Formosans revolted. Nationalist soldiers came from the mainland to put the revolt down. They killed thousands of Formosans, including one of Mr. Yeh's brothers.

Today Mr. Yeh thinks of the Japanese occupation as "the good old days." He has given up speaking Mandarin, except at work, and uses only Japanese at home. He follows the Japanese custom of taking his shoes off before entering a house. He rarely talks politics, even with his family. Once or twice, however, he has said that reunion with Japan might not be a bad idea.

A Formosan Son

Yeh Jinghan \\'jing-hän\\, who is 26, is a foreman in a sugar-refining plant. He barely remembers the Japanese, for he was small when the Nationalists came to Formosa. He used Mandarin in school and studied the writings of Confucius and Dr. Sun Yat-sen. After high school he served in the army for two years. He married soon after leaving the service and has worked in the sugar plant ever since.

Yeh Jinghan's dream is an independent Formosa. He explains the way he feels.

"The Nationalists have always looked down on the Formosans and treated us as if we were second-class citizens. Almost all teachers have come from the mainland. So have most officers in the armed forces, even though more than half the troops are Formosans. A Formosan cannot get a good government job or in any business owned by mainlanders.

"We Formosans have our own history, our own heroes, and our own way of doing things. Independence is the real answer. Then we will be governed by our own officials."

A Mainlander Father

Pai Shi-ming \\'bī-'shi-'ming\\, a 55-year-old general who was born in Nanking, has always been loyal to the Nationalist cause. First, he fought against the Communists in southeast China before they set out on the Long March. Then he fought against the Japanese when they invaded China. During the civil war he fought the Communists again. He came to Formosa in 1949 with Chiang Kai-shek.

General Pai has never felt at home in Formosa. In fact, during his first years on the island, he did not even buy a house and furniture. Any month, he reasoned, the Nationalists would mount an attack against the mainland. As time went on, General Pai did buy land and a large house for himself and wife, his three sons, and their families. But he still feels he is in Formosa only for the time being.

General Pai is convinced the Nationalists can regain control of mainland China. He points out that many farmers there are unhappy with the commune system. He has learned that newspapers and wall posters in Peking sometimes attack certain officials of the Communist party. He views this as a sign that the people are dissatisfied not just with the officials but with communism. "If we invade the mainland," the general says, "the Chinese people are sure to rise up, join us, and overthrow the Communists."

General Pai believes very strongly in the Nationalists. But there is another reason why he dreams of returning to the mainland. He is homesick. He misses Nanking—the broad streets, the green parks, the white and purple lotus flowers that grow in the canals. Before he dies, General Pai wants to live again in the home of his ancestors.

A Mainlander Son

Twenty-four-year-old **Pai Yung-fu** \ˈbī-ˈyùng-ˈfü\ is the oldest of General Pai's three sons. He was born on the mainland and came to Formosa at the age of six. After going through elementary and high school, he attended the National University in Taipei. Then he got a good position in an American-owned plastics company. He is married to a girl who was also born on the mainland. They have one child.

Although Yung-fu shares a household with his parents, he does not share his father's feelings about life on Formosa. Nor does he agree with the general that the Nationalists should attack the mainland. He points out that ferrying troops across the often-stormy Formosa Strait is difficult. He knows also that the Chinese Communist Army is at least five times the size of the Nationalist Army.

He is content with life on the island. He has an interesting job with a good future. He and his wife have visited Japan and look forward to visiting the United States.

He feels that fighting the Communists by example makes more sense than fighting them with soldiers. "The good life that we have on Formosa," he says, "shows that the Nationalists have done better than the Communists. When the people on the mainland realize this, they will throw the Communists out of power. Then the Nationalists will again rule all of China."

What about independence for Formosa as a separate nation? "Never!" says Pai Yung-fu. "We are all Chinese. There can only be one China."

I. Matching Causes and Results

Each statement listed in **Column 1** was the cause of an event listed in **Column 2**. Match the causes and the results.

Column 1

1. Formosa has a fine supply of electric power and labor.
2. Formosa has a warm climate during most of the year.
3. Formosan children attend school for nine years.
4. Some Nationalists consider Formosans to be second-class citizens.

Column 2

a. The main crops are rice, sugar, and pineapples.
b. Most Formosans can read and write.
c. Many Formosans want to be independent.
d. Many industries have developed on Formosa.

II. Questions for Discussion

1. Why are farmers on Formosa so prosperous?
2. How did Japan influence Formosa when it controlled the island?
3. How is the Nationalist government like the Communist government? How is it different?
4. How has the United States helped the Formosan people?
5. In the light of the four views of Formosan life given in your book what do you think the island's future will be?

III. Things to Do

1. Prepare a report on the life of Chiang Kai-shek. Use an encyclopedia to add to the information in your book.
2. Some nations recognize the Communists as the real rulers of China, while others recognize the Nationalists. Look up material about this in an encyclopedia, or write to the United Nations, New York City. Report your findings to the class.

This soldier, who guards the borders of the British crown colony of Hong Kong, gazes across the valley toward Communist China. The slogan painted in Chinese characters on the side of the mountain means "Down with imperialism." The Chinese like to make war with words by using slogans in public places. Britain acquired Hong Kong by treaty in 1842 and has held it as a crown colony ever since. In recent times China has threatened Hong Kong by staging anti-British demonstrations. Thus far, however, Britain has been allowed to hold the colony. China, who does little business with Western nations, benefits from world trade in the free port of Hong Kong. Hong Kong is China's window on the world.

U.P.I. Photo

UNIT 7

China and

In 1949 China's Communists set out on their second Long March. Their goal was a strong and modern nation. Today the Communists are still on the road. According to their leaders it may take as much as 100 years more before they completely reach their goal.

the Road Ahead

FILLING THE RICE BOWLS

The major problem facing China's Communist government is how to feed its people. It is tackling the problem from two directions. It is trying to produce more crops. And it is trying to keep its population from growing so rapidly.

Producing More Crops

Under the so-called commune system, China has succeeded in producing more crops to feed its people. However, it has had trouble with some farmers who would prefer to farm for themselves instead of being commune employees. As a result, the government may have to try still other ways of organizing the farms and farm work.

In the past floods have often destroyed crops and robbed the people of food. To prevent floods, the Communists have built hundreds of earth dams to keep China's rivers within their banks. They are putting up plants to manufacture chemical fertilizers to use instead of manure. And they are setting up agricultural research stations where scientists try to develop seeds that will yield larger crops.

Controlling Population Growth

Growing more crops is only part of the story, however. The important thing is how much food China has compared to its population. China's increase in population is so great that more and more crops must be raised to keep up with it. The best estimates say that at least 40,000 babies arrive in China every day. It means that each year there are about 15,000,000 more mouths to feed. This is a larger number of people than most of the nations of the world have as their total population. It shows the kind of problem that Mr. Tung and China's other farmers must try to meet.

You can see why the Communists are saying that Chinese families should have no more than two children. The government has set up medical centers throughout the country where people can get advice on how to limit their families. It is also urging people not to marry young. A good age for marriage, the government has declared, is 30 for a man and 25 for a woman. The Chinese may decide to have fewer children, but probably not unless each family has a son. It takes a son to carry on the family name, to remember its ancestors, and to care for the parents in their old age.

Sharing Food

In 1959, 1960, and 1961 China had three poor harvests, one after another. One reason was the failure of the commune system. Another reason was bad weather. North China suffered a severe drought, and South China was hit by floods. To meet the problem, the Communists shared available food among all the people. Each Chinese was allowed only certain amounts of grain and meat. In some coastal areas, poor transportation kept food from reaching cities. To feed the city dwellers, the Communists bought large quantities of wheat from foreign countries. They also cut back on certain industrial projects such as automobiles and expanded the production of chemical fertilizers.

So far the Communists have provided food for the people —a thing no other Chinese government has done. For the first time in the nation's long history every Chinese can answer "Yes" to the question, "Have you eaten your rice?" If the time comes when the answer again is "No," there may be a new peasant revolt. Then the Communists will lose the "mandate of Heaven," and a new government will rule.

ENTERING THE WORLD OF MACHINES

When the Red Army entered Peking in 1949, it is said that most of the soldiers saw electric-light bulbs for the first time. To modernize China, the Communist government had to build mills and factories and power plants. It also had to develop a new attitude toward machines because millions of Chinese had no experience with them.

Perhaps the best way to describe how young Chinese feel about machines is to quote from the diary of a worker named **Chen Ing Kwei** \\'chün-'ing-'gwā\\. Ing Kwei grew up on a farm in northwest China. When he was in his teens, the government sent him to school to study automobile mechanics. This is what he wrote.

"The first truck I saw in the country, I saw turning a corner. The driver sat at the steering wheel. I looked through the window and was very happy when I saw how the truck worked. I decided I would make a simple one with a wheel. I said proudly to my friends, 'A man sits in a small room. He turns a wheel and the wheel turns the truck.'

"Then I saw another kind of truck on the road. The exhaust was blowing a lot of smoke out and there was dust and smell. I was very, very happy to see it all. I ran home fast and told my friends, 'I have seen another kind of truck which works different. A man sits in a room and lights a fire and the fire makes smoke which drives the truck.'

"Then one night there came a truck and the lights were on. The lights were very bright. I wondered for a while, 'Oh wonderful! How can they make the oil lamps so bright? How can they set them? Doesn't the oil come out when the truck goes? Oh I wonder how they work!'

"Now the years have gone on and I understand these things. I have driven trucks. I have made light."

China's industries have expanded since 1949. Already China is the second strongest industrial nation in Asia. (Japan is by far the strongest.) However, the Communists are more interested in strengthening China than they are in giving the people a better life. As a result, they have given much attention to such industries as making fertilizers and farm machinery, and to producing electric power and oil. They have paid less attention to producing consumer goods.

KEEPING THE REVOLUTION GOING

If you had lived in China during the school year of 1966-1967, the chances are that you would not have been in school. Instead, you would have been a member of a teen-aged organization called the Red Guards. And you would have spent most of your time "spreading revolution."

The Red Guards

You might have had mimeographed quotations from the writings of Mao Tse-tung and handed them out to passersby. You might have taken a free train ride to a large city and

Chinese Communists make use of demonstrations like this to stir up anti-Western feeling when it suits their purposes. Here the crowd carries posters and Mao's picture. Compare this with a political rally in a democracy.

U.P.I. Photo

marched through the streets with other Red Guards. As you marched, you would shout "Long, long life to Chairman Mao, the reddest red sun in our hearts!" Perhaps you would have criticized a factory manager for not being a good Communist or torn down a street sign because its name was old-fashioned. You might even have smashed Buddhist statues and thrown certain library books into a bonfire.

What was all this about?

A Divided Party

Apparently there are two groups within the Chinese Communist party, and each group has its own ideas. The first group, led by Mao Tse-tung, believes it is more important to "be Red than expert." The second group believes that being expert is just as important as being Red, if not more so.

The first group believes that every person can do all kinds of work. The important thing is to think the right thoughts. As proof, this group points to the Long March and to the years from 1935-1949. At that time people were not only soldiers but also political workers, teachers, and farmers.

This group also wants to wipe out the differences between classes that existed in the past. In Old China, as you recall, people who could read and write looked down on people who worked with their hands. This group of Communists wants educated Chinese today to respect the workers. This is why all Chinese engineers must work as common laborers for a year after graduation. This is why city officials leave their desks at times to do such jobs as loading ships at the docks. Even the highly trained nuclear scientists are expected to leave their laboratories and help farmers harvest crops.

The second group within the Chinese Communist party group points out that it takes experts—people with special training—to run a factory or a mine or to develop an atomic bomb. If experts must spend time working with their hands, they will have less time to spend at their special jobs. And it will take much longer for China to become a strong and modern nation.

Apparently Mao Tse-tung created the Red Guards in an attempt to throw out members who favored the experts in factories, communes, and schools. Also, Mao wanted the young generation to have the same experiences he himself had. He wanted them to struggle against an enemy, just as he had struggled against Chiang Kai-shek and the Nationalists. Hopefully, the young people support his ideas with even greater spirit and enthusiasm.

No one knows whether or not Mao Tse-tung and his followers have been successful. And no one knows what may happen when Mao dies or is no longer in control. The person who succeeds him as head of the party may believe that being Red is more important than being an expert. On the other hand, he may not.

Children of the Revolution

"We are the children of the revolution, sons and daughters of people who were oppressed. We will make ourselves strong with the thinking of our great leader, dear Chairman Mao. We will follow him through storms. We will learn to remove mountains. We will learn to swim by swimming and learn to be true revolutionaries by making revolution."

CHINA AND OTHER NATIONS

The other big problem that faces the Communist government is one that has always troubled China. This is the problem of its relations with other nations.

China's Position in the World

During most of China's long history, its relations with its neighbors were very much like the relations between the Chinese emperor and the Chinese people. The emperor set an example for his people, and China set an example for its neighbors. Korea, for instance, borrowed the Chinese writing system. Japan borrowed China's writing system and its style of painting. The Chinese were respectful toward the emperor, and neighboring nations were respectful toward China. They paid tribute to show that they were inferior. When their ambassadors appeared at the emperor's court, they knelt and bowed their heads to the ground three times. This is called "kowtowing."

At times China was weak. Either nomads from the North invaded the country, or the government was divided. Then China's boundaries shrank. At other times, however, China was strong. And whenever it was strong, it extended its territory as far as it could to the north, west, and south.

In the middle of the 1800's foreign businessmen gained special rights in certain Chinese cities. Europeans controlled most of the nation's banks, factories, mines, and railroads. China lost territory to Japan and Russia. It might even have been completely divided if foreign powers had been able to agree on the division.

After the fall of the Chinese empire, Sun Yat-sen, Chiang Kai-shek, and Mao Tse-tung had different ideas about developing New China. But all agreed that China must be independent and strong and once again a leader in Asia.

The Communists, under Mao's leadership, have established China as one of the two most powerful Communist nations in the world. They have done this by building up some industries, by developing atomic weapons, and by a show of military strength at various times in Asia.

One of Mao's first military actions was taken against Tibet, a mountainous region on China's border with India. This Buddhist country had been a part of China during the Manchus. After the Chinese republic was established in 1912, the Nationalists allowed Tibet to govern itself under

The people of Tibet are believers in Lamaism, a special form of Buddhism. Their ruler before the Chinese Communists took over Tibet was their chief monk, the Dalai Lama. The Buddha shown here stands in a Lama temple in Peking. Can you see why it is sometimes called the "Smiling" Buddha?

Sawders from Cushing

its chosen ruler, a Buddhist monk. Late in 1950 the Chinese Communists decided to re-establish their rule over Tibet. Communist troops moved into the region. They soon captured the capital and forced Tibet's young ruler to accept Chinese "protection."

The Chinese Communists then began to make Tibet a real part of China. They built roads and airfields and sent Chinese into Tibet to teach communism. The Tibetans tried to revolt, but the Chinese brutally crushed the revolt, killing many thousands. During this period the Tibetan ruler, fearing for his life, fled to India and was given refuge. Taking over Tibet seemed natural to the Chinese because it had once belonged to the Chinese empire. But people all over the world—and especially some Asian countries—were shocked by the brutality of the Chinese troops and by China's growing power.

The Chinese considered India's hospitality to Tibet's ruler as the act of an enemy. When trouble arose on the border between India and Tibet, Chinese troops staged a surprise attack against the Indian army. The Indians were unprepared and soon retreated. After this show of force the Communists declared a cease-fire and withdrew. But they continued to hold the territory their troops had overrun and which India claimed. Chinese and Indian troops engage in battles along the border from time to time. But India is not strong enough to push the Chinese out.

Aggressive actions of this kind by the Chinese have caused some Asian nations to fear them. Many rulers are careful not to oppose China. Because of this the United States has come to their aid. It has made treaties with China's non-Communist neighbors and built military bases to guard against a Communist take-over.

Mao and his associates believe that communism is destined to become world wide. They aspire to lead the Communist

U.P.I. Photo

Militant war posters like this one, which faces Canton's main railway station, are very popular in China today as a way of teaching Communist ideas.

movement, especially among the underdeveloped nations. They resent the United States and the Soviet Union and are trying to build China into a third great power capable of challenging them. Let us see how the Chinese regard the two great nations which are so powerful that they can block China's expansion.

China and the United States

The Chinese make use of the theater, opera, and movies to show their hatred of their enemies. The chief villain is always Chiang Kai-shek. Next to Chiang, the Chinese dislike the United States. Sometimes the United States is shown as a soldier attacking unarmed farmers. Sometimes it is shown as a banker piling up money while poor people starve. Such scenes always call forth boos from the audience and sometimes even cries of "Sha! Sha!"—"Kill! kill!"

One reason why the Chinese resent and fear the United States is the military treaties which it has formed with some Asian nations. They feel that Americans are trying to surround them with military bases and to play a role in Asia that they consider rightfully theirs.

Another reason why the Chinese dislike the United States is that it does not recognize the Communists as China's real rulers. The United States supports the Nationalists, whom the Communists drove from the mainland in 1949, and has given them much help. Chiefly because of American efforts, Communist China has not been voted membership in the United Nations. Instead one of the seats of the permanent "Big Five" is held by Nationalist China (along with the United States, Britain, France, and the Soviet Union). Nationalist China gained this important place in the United Nations because it fought with the Western powers in World War II.

Some Americans disagree with the United States policy on Communist China. They point out that the Communists rule 750,000,000 Chinese, while the Nationalists rule only 13,500,000. Moreover, it is not likely that the Nationalists can reconquer the mainland. These people feel that the Communists should be recognized as China's rightful rulers and that Red China should be allowed to join the United Nations.

Most Americans, however, think that recognizing Communist China would mean overlooking its warlike movements against Tibet and India. This would also mean betraying Asian nations that oppose communism. And it might encourage Communist revolts in such nations as Thailand, Malaysia, and perhaps even India. These Americans say that no action should be taken to help a Communist government gain more power.

China and the Soviet Union

China and the Soviet Union are the world's largest and most important Communist nations. For a number of years they were friends. But this is no longer so. Today each aspires to be the leader of world communism. Each accuses the other of various stupidities. The chief difference between the two is that the Chinese still follow Marx and his ideas of world revolution. The Russians, on the other hand, have declared a policy of "peaceful co-existence" in dealing with non-Communist countries.

One week Soviet newspapers describe China's leaders as stupid and backward. The next week a Chinese official replies by calling the Soviet leaders "a gang of national scums and traitors." Every few months an anti-Chinese demonstration takes place in Moscow or an anti-Russian parade in Peking.

Sometimes there are bursts of gunfire along the 3,800 miles of common border. The reason for this is a dispute over boundaries. If you should compare a Russian map of the Soviet Union with one published in Peking, you would discover differences in two areas. One region is north of Sinkiang. The other lies north of what was once called Manchuria. The Russian map shows these areas as part of the Soviet Union. Peking's map shows them as part of China. Actually, these areas were part of China from the late 1600's to the middle of the 1800's. Then China gave these border lands to Russia. However, the Chinese Communists say that China gave up this land only because it was too weak to resist foreign soldiers. Now China is stronger, so it wants its former territory back.

Another reason why the two Communist nations quarrel is that Russian armies occupied Manchuria just before the end of World War II. When Japan surrendered, the Russian troops pulled out and turned the countryside over to the Chinese Communists. But they gave the cities to the Nationalists. However, they took with them all the factory equipment they could carry. They needed the machines to replace their own destroyed in the war. The Chinese Communists deeply resented these actions of the Russians because they also needed the machines.

To make matters worse, the Russians advised Mao Tsetung to disband the Red Army and join Chiang Kai-shek. They believed that Mao would lose the struggle with the Nationalists. The Chinese Communists were insulted by this advice.

After the Communists took over mainland China in 1949, the Russians agreed to help them. Russian engineers were sent to show Chinese workers how to use modern machines. Chinese students studied in Moscow. The two nations seemed very close.

Gradually Moscow and Peking began to develop different ideas about communism. They both agreed that communism was the best form of government, but they disagreed about how to make it work. For example, the Chinese set up communes to help increase farm crops. The Russians said that communes would never work. As it turned out, the Russians were right. But the Chinese did not like the Russians saying, "We told you so."

Also, the Russians had already built up such industries as chemicals, electric-power production, oil, and farm machinery. Now they were turning their attention to producing consumer goods, such as textiles and automobiles. The Chinese, who were far behind the Russians in industry, could not afford to do this. It was much more important for their farmers to have enough fertilizer than for people to have two suits of clothes. The Chinese felt the Russians were betraying communism by paying attention to the welfare of individuals rather than the welfare of the nation.

For many years the Soviet Union was the leader of world communism because communism had its beginning there.

After World War II the Russians took over several neighboring countries and set up Communist governments in them. These countries were completely under Russian control and remained so for a number of years. Then Yugoslavia, in central Europe, began to pull away in a desire to manage its own affairs. Finally it succeeded and no longer followed Moscow's bidding.

The Chinese too began to act independently of the Soviet Union. They claimed that they were superior to the Russians because they followed the teachings of Marx more closely. Mao believed that his plans were better suited to world revolution than Russia's were. He began to send his agents and experts not only into the neighboring countries of southeast Asia but to Africa and Latin America as well.

In 1960 the Russians apparently decided to show China who was the leader of the Communist world. They called their engineers back to Moscow, an action that hurt China's budding industries greatly. For several years many factories stood idle while the Chinese tried to figure out how to operate the Russian-designed machines and how to replace the Russian-built parts.

Since then the Chinese have learned to be self-sufficient. They became even more independent after they developed atomic weapons. Mao and his group accused the Russians of betraying the principles of communism. China has refused to attend meetings of the Communist nations called by the Russians in an effort to reestablish their leadership.

Today the Chinese believe they are the true exponents of communism. They will build communism at home. And they will spread it through the underdeveloped nations of the world. Even more important China wants to set an example for other nations as it once did long ago. These are the things that China plans to do in its second Long March.

I. Recognizing True and False Statements

Some of the following sentences are **true**. Some are **not true**. Rewrite each false statement correctly in your notebook.

1. Using chemical fertilizers can increase crop production.
2. Girls are as welcome as boys in a Chinese family.
3. The Chinese Communist government considers steel mills more important than textile factories.
4. The communes were a great success.
5. The Chinese are trying to increase population.
6. Communist China fears the United States.
7. All Communist nations try to help one another.
8. Communist China has lived at peace with its neighbors.
9. Thinking the right thoughts, according to Mao Tse-tung, is more important than know-how.

II. Questions for Discussion

1. Why were the Red Guards organized? Give two reasons.
2. How does the government influence education in China?
3. How does the government find out about the lives of its citizens? Explain why it does this.
4. Why are Communist China and the Soviet Union not as friendly as they once were?

III. Making Comparisons

1. Compare Communist China's progress in industry and in science with that of the Soviet Union. Consult an encyclopedia or current magazines to find this information and report to the class.
2. Compare life in Communist China with life in the United States in respect to (a) freedom to speak, (b) freedom to choose a job, (c) freedom to read, and (d) freedom to vote for public officials.

Glossary

The glossary contains the words and terms whose meanings and pronunciations you may want to refer to. The page number after each definition tells where the word is used.

The following is a key* to the special spellings used after the words in the glossary and in the text.

a as in mat	ch as in chin	ng as in sing
ā as in age	e as in bet	ō as in bone
ä as in cart	ē as in even	ȯ as in corn
aù as in sound	i as in tip	ü as in rule
	ī as in side	

ə as in banana, perplex, capital, color, supper

A slant line is placed at the beginning and the end of each word. An accent appears **before** the accented syllable. An accent at the top of a letter is the primary, or strong, accent. An accent below a letter is a secondary, or weak, accent.

ancestors \\'an-ˌses-tərz\\: Forefathers, such as grandparents, great grandparents, and so on, 13

antimony \\'ant-ə-ˌmō-nē\\: A metallic element used in pigments, as in printing, 106

archaeologists \\är-ke-'äl-ə-jəsts\\: Scientists who dig in the earth to learn about the past, 10

bamboo: A treelike grass that grows in warm lands, 12

bronze: A mixture, or alloy, made of copper and tin, 9

Bronze Age: Prehistoric period when men used bronze tools, 9

Buddhism \\'bü-diz-əm\\: A religion brought from India to China, 17

caravan \\'kar-ə-van\\: A train of pack animals, 59

ceramics \\sə-'ram-iks\\: Pottery or porcelain objects, 54

charms: Paper inscriptions supposed to ward off illness, 62

chin-shih \\'jin-'shir\\: A person who passed the civil-service examinations in order to qualify for public office, 50

civil-service system: Plan of selecting public officials through competitive examinations, 51

collective \\kə'lek-tiv\\: A large farm formed of many small farms operated as a single unit under government supervision

*The system of indicating pronunciation is used by permission. From *Webster's New Elementary Dictionary*, copyright 1965 by G. & C. Merriam Co., Publishers of the Merriam-Webster Dictionaries.

commune \\'käm-ˌyün\\: A large collectived farm in Communist China where people work and live under strict government rules

cooperative \\kō-'äp-ə-rət-iv\\: A large farm made of many small farms, operated by the farmers themselves, who shared the harvest according to the amount of land, tools, and animals each contributed

Confucianism \\kən-'fyü-shən-izm\\: Belief in the teachings of Confucius, 15

dialect \\'dī-ə-ˌlect\\: Speech that differs from the standard speech, 47

dynasty \\'dī-nə-stē\\: Succession of rulers of the same family, 10

gorge \\'gȯrj\\: A narrow passage between mountains, 38

guerrilla \\gə'ril-ə\\ **warfare:** Attacks by troops who make surprise raids behind enemy lines, 83

hutungs \\hu-'dùnz\\: Streets in the old sections of Peking, 100

jade \\'jād\\: A hard stone used to carve ornamental objects, 56

k'ang: A kind of stove used in winter as a bed, 11

Kuomintang \\'guō-'min-'däng\\: National People's Party in China, 79

land reform: System of land redistribution among peasants, 86

legation \\li-'gā-shən\\: Official residence and office of a high official of a foreign government, 77

loess \\'les\\: The fine, soft soil on the Yellow River plain, 34

monsoons \\män-'sünz\\: Seasonal winds that blow across Asia, 32

movable type: Separate characters or letters that can be put together to form words or sentences in printing, 63

nomads \\'nō-madz\\: People who wander from place to place without a permanent home, 18

opium \\'ō-pē-əm\\: A habit-forming drug made of poppies, 73

overseas Chinese: Chinese who live in other countries, 79

parapet \\'par-ə-pet\\: Low wall to protect soldiers, 66

peace treaty: Agreement between nations ending a war, 74

sampan \\'sam-pan\\: A small flat-bottomed houseboat, 39

shan-shui \\'shän-'shü-ē\\: Chinese landscape painting, 56

Stone Age: Prehistoric period when men used stone tools, 9

tariff: Government tax on exports and imports, 74

terraces: Steps cut into hillsides to provide more crop land, 33

treaty port: Port open to foreign trade according to agreement, 70

tribute: Money paid by one ruler or nation to another to secure some sort of privilege, 70

tungsten: A metallic element used in making steel, 106

warlords: Military leaders who formerly held power in local districts in China and held it by force, 80

Index

Ancestors, respect for, 12-13, 22-23
Anshan, 106
Anyang, 10
Archaeologists, 10
Architecture, in Old China, 64
Art, in Old China, 53-59

"Big Five," in United Nations, 148
Boxer Rebellion, 76-77
Bronze Age, 9, 10
Buddhism, in China, 17, 142; in Tibet, 145-146

Canton, 44, 70-71, 73-,74, 75
Canton, trade with Europe, 70-71, 71-74
Censorship, in Communist China, 119-120
Ch'in dynasty, 15-17
China, and United States, 147-148; and Soviet Union, 148-151, and world revolution, 149
Chiang Kai-shek, 81-83, 87-88, 123, 131, 133, 143, 144, 147
Chinese empire, established, 3, 16; growth of, 17, 18; fall of, 78-80, 144
Chinese language and writing, 11, 46, 48-49, 76
Chou dynasty, 11-12
Ch'u Yuan, poet, 129
Christianity, in China, 77
Chungking, 37, 38, 44, 100
Cities, of China, 44, 100-103
Civil service, in Old China, 49, 51-52
Classes, in Old China, 22-27
Communes, life on, 94-100
Communist Manifesto, 86, 112-113
Communist party, organization, 110-111; division within, 114; 142-143
Communists, beliefs of, 111-113, 142-143; and land reform, 86; and Red Army, 1-2, 3, 86, 113-114, 139

Confucianism, 15, 17
Confucius, 3, 13-15, 16, 48-50, 54, 78, 130

Dragon Boat Festival, 129
Dutch, on Formosa, 130

Education in Communist China, 87, 114-120, 142; in Formosa, 126, 134
Engels, Friedrich, 112, 113

Family life, in Old China, 22-27; in Communist China, 95-99, 103-105
Festivals and holidays, in Communist China, 104, 109; on Formosa, 128-130
Formosa, 88, 122-134
Formosa Strait, 131, 134

Gobi, desert, 36
Government, in Old China, 51-53, 75; of Communist China, 109-111
Grand Canal, 3, 43-44, 70
Great Britain, trade with China, 71-72, 75; war with, 73-74
Great Wall, 3, 16, 64-66
Gunpowder, invented, 3, 63-64, 76

Han dynasty, 17, 87
Hong Kong, 74, 78
Hwang Ho (Yellow River), 8, 41-42, 43, 108

Ichang, 38
India, and Chinese aggression, 145, 146, 148
Industry, in Communist China, 106-109, 139-140; on Formosa, 124-125, 127-128
Inner Mongolia, 35

Japan, adoption of Chinese ways, 76-77, 144; aggression against China, 5, 83-84; defeat, 87, 106, 149; on Formosa, 125, 131-132

Kao-hsiung, Formosa city, 127
Kirun, harbor of, 132

155

Korea, adoption of Chinese writing, 76, 144
Koxinga, General, 129-130
Kublai Khan, 18, 19, 69
Kuomintang, 79, 80, 85, 130, 131

Land reform, on China mainland, 86; on Formosa, 125
Lin Yutang, quoted, 27
Loess Highlands, 34
Long March, of Communists, 1-3, 87, 113, 117, 133, 142

Manchu dynasty, 20, 70, 71, 73, 74, 78-80, 84, 86-88, 109, 112
Mandarin, 47-49, 115, 132
Mao Tse-tung, 84, 86-88, 109, 112, 113, 142, 143, 144, 145
Marriage, in Communist China, 138-139; in Old China, 27
Marx, Karl, 111-113
Ming dynasty, 20, 87
Marco Polo, 3-4, 18, 19, 69-70, 77, 106,
Manchuria, 83, 84, 88, 106
Money, coining of, 12
Mongolian People's Republic, 36
Mukden, 106

Nanking, 78, 83, 88, 134
Nationalist China. See Formosa.
Nationalists, and Sun Yat-sen, 79, 81; and Chiang's army, 1, 5, 81-82, 83-84, 88; overthrow of, 85-88
Natural resources of mainland China, 106-109; of Formosa, 128
New Year's, Chinese, 128-129
North China, 31, 34-35, 38, 44

Opium War, 73-75
Outer China, 31, 35-36

Paper, invented, 3, 17, 61-63, 76
Paper money, 3, 18
Peking, 44, 77, 86, 88, 100-105, 139, 149
People's Republic of China, birth of, 88, 109-110

Pottery and porcelain, developed, 3, 7, 9, 17, 55
Population, of Old China, 72; of Communist China, 138-139
Printing, invented, 3, 18, 62-63, 76
Portuguese, trade with China, 4, 70

Red Army, 113-114, 139
Red Guards, 141-143
Republic of China, 122-134

Shang dynasty, 10-11, 46
Shanghai, 40, 74, 76-77, 83, 87, 100
Shih Huang Ti, 16-17, 64, 66
Silk, production of, 3, 59-61, 76
Silk Road, ancient, 59
South China, 31, 32-33, 40, 44, 100
Soviet Union, and Sun Yat sen, 81; and Communist China, 148-151
Stone Age, in China, 9, 10
Sui dynasty, 43
Sung dynasty, 18
Sun Yat-sen, 78-81, 99, 132

Taipei, 130, 131, 134
Taiwan. See Formosa.
T'ang dynasty, 18, 54-55
Theater, in Old China, 58-59
Tibet, 35-37, 40, 145-146, 148
Tiensin, 44
Tsinling Mountains, 31, 32

United Nations, and China, 148
United States, aid to Nationalists, 125, 127, 128; as mediator, 87-88; and Communist China, 146, 147-148; and Seventh Fleet, 131

World War II, Nationalists in, 84, 148
Wuhan, 38-39, 44, 106

Yangtze Kiang, 12, 37-40, 41, 43, 72, 74, 83, 106, 108
Yellow River, plain and valley, 8, 41, 42, 44. See also Hwang Ho.
Yenan, 2
Young Pioneers, 115, 116
Yuan Shih-kai, 79-80, 88

156